Thinking with the Heart

Publisher: Tamara Traeder
Editorial Director: Roy M. Carlisle
Marketing Director: Carol Brown
Art Director: Leyza Yardley
Production Coordinator: Larissa Berry
Cover Design: Jeff Wincapaw
Interior Design and Typesetting: Margaret Copeland/Terragraphics

Typographic Specifications: Text in Hoefler Text 11/18, headings in Hiroshige Book.

Printed in the United States of America

Library of Congress Cataloging-in-Publication Data
McCarroll, Tolbert.
    Thinking with the heart : a monk (and parent) explores his Christian heritage / Tolbert McCarroll.
        p.cm.
    ISBN 1-879290-21-9
        1. Spiritual life--Catholic Church. I. Title.

BX2350.3 .M33 2001
248.4'82--dc21

2001034607

Distributed to the trade by FaithWorks,
a division of National Book Network

10 9 8 7 6 5 4 3 2 1   01 02 03 04 05

To the memory of
Issa
Viola Pecquet McCarroll
Etty Hillesum
Paul Monette
and all the beauty and love that
has come before me

And in appreciation of
Mary Martha Aggeler
Julian DeRossi
and all who have shared and made
possible my journey and my time

And to the hope in
David
Holly
Andrew
and all the beauty and love
that will come after me

Contents

New Paths Through an Old Meadow

When my mother was approaching seventy she began crocheting colorful squares. She wanted to give me something of her best craft before her eyesight failed. After several years, there were enough squares for her to put them together into an afghan. She was blind when she died at eighty-five. During the winter months, this much appreciated afghan is on my bed.

Like my mother's afghan, this book is made up of little squares of spiritual experience. Who am I? Much of my life story is in the final chapter of the book. I am a seventy-year-old lay monk living in a small community. I am also an adoptive parent of three young children: fifteen-year-old David, eleven-year-old Holly, and nine-year-old Andrew. For a number of years, I have been involved with children who have special needs. Many of them have had their lives made difficult by the AIDS pandemic. Some of these children have been at home and nearby, others were in Romania, quite a few are in Uganda. I have learned much about spiritual growth from each of these children.

In the twenty-first century, the religious structures I have known for seventy years will, most likely, fade away. Whatever has been experienced as oppressive or limiting in the Western religious traditions will no longer restrict people's lives. Yet the need for each of us to be spiritually nourished will continue. In part, this book is my spiritual will and testament to my children, to you, and to all who are willing to claim the common spiritual legacy to be found in these pages.

Is there anything in my experience, as a person primarily of the twentieth century, that can beneficially be shared with those of you who must work to focus the spiritual energies of the age to come? I think so.

For me, World War II was the pivotal event of the twentieth century. Spiritually, the Holocaust was at the center of that event. And someplace shining in that center was the writer Etty Hillesum. Etty was born in 1914, fifteen years before me. I have come to regard her as a spiritual older sister. We were both trained as lawyers, but beyond that our lives were very different. She was Dutch and I am American. She grew up in an assimilated Jewish environment; my family were devout Catholics. During the 1940s she was part of the movement in Europe exploring the bond between psychology and spirituality. It was not until the 1960s, in California, that I discovered and connected with similar explorers. These differences between us do not matter much. There are some fundamental spiritual attitudes that bind me to her and which I hope are reflected in the pages that follow.

What I respect most is that Etty Hillesum used her own experience to seek, and find, the divine even in the darkest of circumstances and people. Also, she searched for God and beauty primarily in the details of her everyday life. And, even when "everyday" meant life in a concentration camp, she was an apostle of the need for love—always.

Etty was murdered at Auschwitz on November 30, 1943. She was twenty-nine. Two years before she was killed she reflected in her diary on where we all were as a spiritual people, why we have such insecurity, and what we have to do.

> Many people have fixed ideas, and so they bring their children up in rigid ways. The result is not enough freedom of action. With us it was precisely the other way round. I think my parents always felt out of their depth, and as life became more and more difficult they were gradually so overwhelmed that they became quite incapable of making up their minds about anything. They gave us children too much freedom of action, and offered us nothing to cling to.

That was because they never established a foothold for themselves. And the reason why they did so little to guide our steps was that they themselves had lost the way.

And I see our own task more and more clearly: to allow their roving talents to mature and take more solid shape in us, their children.[1]

Etty's insight was also a prediction of a condition that became more and more pervasive in the prosperous post-war period and continues today. But there have been many who have worked at establishing "a foothold for themselves" and encouraged the "roving talents" of our age "to mature and take more solid shape." Certainly Etty herself was one of them.

The pages of this book contain some spiritual footholds that have been pointed out to me and which I have found helpful. But at this point I have to switch metaphors for my image is not climbing a spiritual mountain but strolling across a meadow. Here Etty's footholds become stepping stones into a sacred space. As a child, my space was a protective enclosure: family, church, school. Now I imagine that space as a wide and wonderful meadow with fascinating variations. John Moschos wrote a charming book around A.D. 600. He called it *The Spiritual Meadow*. After painting a lovely picture of flowers in many colors he writes:

I have titled this work "meadow" because of the delight, the fragrance, and the benefit which it will give to those who walk across it.[2]

There is an old official path across the meadow of our spiritual heritage, and it is still recommended by some. That old path is worn out and not very inviting to most people. But the meadow itself is fresh and vibrant, always growing and changing. It would be a tragic mistake to abandon the meadow when we reject the old path. There can be many new refreshing paths into this magnificent landscape.

This book is an invitation to explore. My hope is that it will contribute to the spiritual growth of some who will find their way in life as free women and men.

TOUCHING THE DIVINE

Thinking with the Heart

e do not need more religious knowledge. The forty-eighth chapter of the ancient Chinese scripture *Tao Te Ching*[3] cautions that although in the pursuit of knowledge "every day something is added" in the quest for spirituality, in the sacred way, "every day something is dropped." How refreshing it would have been if Sister Muriel, the nun who taught my fifth-grade religion class, would have asked; "Well, class, what facts have you unlearned and discarded today?" Never did such a thing happen in the history of Catholic education.

As a young child I prayed by talking to God. Rarely did I simply listen for God. But somehow, like everyone else, I did eventually learn to value moments of stillness. Through the years these became of increasing necessity for me. Technological and social revolutions have accelerated the pace of change during my lifetime. Adapting to such rapid transitions has been difficult. Like others, I often feel an imbalance in my life and a desire to find a quiet stillpoint in the midst of events that at times seem out of control.

In the 1960s I joined many people in the Western world who had a growing spiritual yearning and looked eastward for comfort. It was an exciting time of experimentation. We tended to move with fascination from one spiritual import to another. It was fun but sometimes shallow. I often found myself playacting. I bought a meditation pillow and imagined myself a Japanese Zen Buddhist. Attracted to the serenity and wisdom of Tibetan teachers, I wondered if I had not known them in some earlier existence. At various times I was also pretending to be a Hopi, a Sufi, and a Shaker. After a few months with each new discipline, there was an inevitable awkwardness, and I had to separate adventure from authentic experience.

My inner needs are never satisfied by attempting to import a spirituality from a different cultural environment. Some people are able to transcend their backgrounds, but many of us are not. However, my cross-cultural spiritual experiences have been grafted onto my own cultural roots for which I am grateful. Some Eastern approaches to spiritual concepts have been very helpful to me.

Chinese ancients, for example, accepted two kinds of thinking. I have found this distinction useful. The rational mind is appropriate for logical thoughts. But in the realm of the intuitive, another process is needed. This was sometimes described as "thinking with the heart." I love this concept, which was portrayed in pictographic language as a square with an arrow shooting through it. Our wisdom is like that arrow which, in a flash, can transcend the quagmire of convoluted mental concepts.

I distinguish my religion from my spiritual growth. Religion can be troubling when associated with institutions, dogma, and politics. The word "religion" comes from the Latin *religare*, which means to bind back or anchor. I have the image of something which keeps a little boat from drifting out of control in conflicting currents. Having access to age-old teachings can be useful. But it is not enough to talk about the sacred. It must also be experienced.

Our word "spiritual" derives from the Latin *spirare*, meaning to breathe or blow. *Spirare* also describes the animating agent that gives life to creatures and that has sometimes been translated simply as "the breath of life." Many languages have words that imitate breath: *chi* in Chinese, *psyche* in Greek. The fact that there was an actual sound connected with the spiritual suggests it was quite real to the ancients. While religion may offer me an understanding of existence, spirituality is a refreshing invitation to experience the breath of life.

As I was preparing this book, I received a telephone call from a young TV producer working on a proposal for a program to be called "The Future of Faith." Because his associates had produced a successful documentary on Pope John Paul II, I assumed, incorrectly, that he was exploring the future of Christian institutions. He listened to my thoughts and then said, "People my age are not looking for a church." He is right. If we, young and old, are not looking for a religious institution in our faith journeys, what are we seeking?

"Faith" is a difficult term. There are very few references to it in the Old Testament. In contrast, Paul's letters in the New Testament allude to the concept two hundred times. To Christians, "faith" quickly came to mean revealed truth that has to be accepted—and church leaders are to decide what is authentic revelation. I don't think there is much future there. But "faith" can also mean confidence. I trust, for example, that God is with us in the life we share with each other. Others are more comfortable expressing the same concept in a different way. The vocabulary does not matter. Many, if not most of us, have confidence that we are each able to encounter a transcendent reality. No one person has the whole truth about this spiritual process.

The same young producer who declared that people his age were not looking for a church eschewed his generation's race for power, wealth, and privilege. He found no hope in the gods of commercialism and consumerism. "We must," he said, "make time to listen to other people's spiritual stories." That, it struck me, was not only a beautiful thought but an essential one. It is from the spiritual journeys of others that we catch glimpses of the many facets of the sacred in our world. In the pages that follow, I will share some lessons I have learned from a number of people, most of whom have religious backgrounds that are quite different from mine. The journeys we make as seekers are more important than the destinations we reach from time to time.

As I stumble around with the ordinary tasks of life, I often sense that I have one foot in the realm of the spiritual. At times, I worry about words. At other times, I don't. On some nights, as I look at the sky, it fills me with awe to realize that the earth was formed from the dust of exploding stars and that each of us is composed of atoms from the stars. Stardust is my essential being. At these moments, my faith simply means respecting my stardust.

The older I get the more I long to learn from musicians, poets, artists, and others who move beyond obvious and measurable factual forms. They reshape the world in order to give a more authentic picture of life. A musician can transpose a song from one key to another and change our ability to sing it. There are moments, often little ones I think, which can transpose our existence into a different spiritual key.

2

Sharing the Song

Three important events in my faith journey came from my association with some Shaker sisters, an Italian art historian, and a dying cellist.

The spiritual process is close to music. There are healing and refreshing songs in each of us, in our history, environment, relationships, dreams, and prayers. The Hopi people in Arizona sing,

And the bird's song,
and the people's song,
and the song of life,
will all become one.

It's true. In this song of life we each have notes to sing.

Some important spiritual songs have been in the custody of various religious institutions where they have been safeguarded and refined over the centuries. But an institution is only the custodian; it does not own the song. The Shakers taught me this many years ago.

Shaker spirituality and music had long fascinated me. I assumed all the Shakers were dead, and was surprised to find a small but vital surviving community in Sabbathday Lake, Maine. A correspondence began. In the late 1960s, when my own spiritual community was forming, two of us accepted an invitation to visit the Shakers. One evening we were sitting around the great stove in the Sabbathday Lake kitchen. Sister Frances had baked gingerbread from an old recipe. This led us into a discussion of other treasures from the past. I had been reluctant to mention that we used their hymns in our services. I thought they might consider it presumptuous for non-Shakers to make use of these songs. When I did tell them, they wholeheartedly approved of our doing it. Eighty-year-old Sister Mildred promptly asked us to name a favorite and to sing it. We sang *'Tis The Gift To Be Simple*. When we finished, we asked if we were doing it the right way. "Oh, yes," said Sister Mildred, "you sing it the right way." The other sisters nodded and smiled. I was amazed we had sung it properly. Sensing my thoughts, Sister Frances said, "We sing it a different way, but both ways are the right way." In that instant I realized that notes and interpretation were not the essence of a Shaker song. The sisters were concerned about the spiritual experience when the song was sung. The sisters taught us to sing many other songs that night. There was no sense of owning or controlling the songs that are so uniquely associated with the Shaker tradition. As we were leaving, Sister Mildred said, "Now we know God has put a little Shaker spark in you." I have never doubted it. Nor have I ever forgotten the humility with which they shared their spiritual heritage.

My own Catholic community has guarded and refined many spiritual rhythms in the past two millennia. Unlike the Shakers at Sabbathday Lake, Catholic churchmen have sometimes misunderstood their role as custodians and become too possessive. Four hundred years ago, at the time of the Reformation, they were forced to relinquish an exclusive claim to the sacraments and other harmonies between the divine and the human. This has made it easier in our own age to understand that every person is entitled to sing the songs coming out of the Catholic tradition. To me, this openness must be included in any definition of "catholic." The Greek *katholikos* means "universal" or, when broken down even more, "concerning the whole." Whatever spiritual gifts we have, they are for the whole—everyone who can make use of them.

Forty years ago I was taught another important lesson about spiritual heritage. My teacher was an Italian woman. We met in Milan. She was introduced simply as "Miss

Linda," an art historian with a special interest in spirituality. Her intent was to instruct me on some facets of Renaissance painting and religion. To illustrate a point, she took me and a friend who served as interpreter to view a particular fresco in a nearby church. When we arrived at the chapel containing the painting, we were stopped by a chained grill. Miss Linda promptly summoned a guard. He brashly told her the chapel was never opened at this time of day, and, in addition, it had recently been closed indefinitely by order of the cardinal-archbishop. He pointed to official notices wired to the grill. Miss Linda was a small, shy, and quite humble person. The guard was big and filled with his own importance. To me the issue was closed. I was about to reassure her that our coming was no inconvenience to me when she began an amazing lecture.

Miss Linda told the guard that neither he nor the cardinal owned the Catholic heritage and therefore they were not entitled to stand between the treasures of that tradition and those who sought nourishment from them. She then went on to point out to him, gently but with great authority, that he was unaware of the spiritual process he was presuming to interrupt. She spoke of the forces that inspired the painting and the spiritual needs of those of us standing at this locked grill. She ended with the simple statement that she was a part of the living history of religion and he had no right to block her way.

The guard looked at Miss Linda for a long moment. Then, without a word, he reached in his pocket for the keys. The grill swung open. Miss Linda entered the chapel. In great awe, I followed. I do not remember what I learned from the fresco, but I have never forgotten Miss Linda's confrontation with the guard. The churches are human institutions which serve useful purposes in protecting the spiritual songs. But they must share their gifts freely with the whole "People of God," a good phrase coming out of the Second Vatican Council in 1964. God's people, said the council, have existed "at all times and in every race."

Many of us hear a spiritual song before we ever find God. Some never find God. I'm not so sure it matters. This is how I felt with my friend Colin.

Colin Hampton (1911-1996) was a remarkable cellist, composer, and teacher. I met Colin in the last years of his long life. He was a generous man who would do anything for a young musician. He had little admiration for organized religion, but to those who knew him best there was always a deep spirituality behind the secular mask. In midlife, for example, Colin visited a remote Scottish island. Years later he composed a moving piece, "The Ring of Brodgar," for six cellos. He prefaced it with words he, and his son Ian, had written, which reveal Colin's spiritual perspective:

Above the fishing village of Stromness on the main island of Orkney, Scotland, stands the Ring of Brodgar. This 5000 year old circle of Unhewn Sandstone Monoliths stands bleakly on a plateau where the constant winds discourage the growth of anything higher than the heather that carpets the hills. The Orkneys are steeped in pre-history so that a visit to this lonely site persuades a modern visitor of the Power of the Unknown and of the formidable achievements of his ancient ancestors.

As a boy, Colin was a chorister at Westminster Abbey on a merit scholarship. He did not care for the life much, but some of the music had a profound effect on him. Colin moved on as soon as possible to the Royal Academy of Music. For thirty-six years, he was cellist in the internationally acclaimed Griller Quartet. Later he was a professor of music at the University of California in Berkeley.

Nearing eighty-five and in bad health, Colin began to tidy up the loose ends of his life. A mutual friend brought us together because Colin wanted to think of himself as one of the people of God but had "trouble with belief."

Colin had been the hands of God in bringing music into the world. The task for me was to help Colin feel that a musical partnership with the divine was, in God's eyes, more important than "belief."

Together we explored life, which is, as someone said, "a mystery to be lived not a problem to be solved." The same is certainly true of faith. Theologians get into the metaphysics of mysteries. For most of us that is not a fruitful pursuit.

When Colin challenged me to share my own faith, I realized that, to me, it is a way of experiencing the holy in life. In the process, I can understand and be comfortable with incomplete and evolving concepts of God, Jesus, death, grace, prayer, and many other issues. I assumed that musicians face the same thing. For example, to what extent is it necessary to understand every inner facet of Beethoven's being before playing Beethoven? And, I asked Colin, is it not true that only by playing Beethoven can a person begin to understand Beethoven? Colin was amused with my crude attempt to use his passion for music in my spiritual arguments. But, he acknowledged, the comparison was not without merit. He began to relax on the issue of beliefs. Together we encouraged each other to play God's music now and understand the composer later—or never.

Ian Hampton writes in his afterword to his father's memoirs, "For Colin, composition was a spiritual quest."[4] In the last months of his life Colin composed a beautiful setting for John Donne's (1572-1631) "Sacred Sonnets," written for tenor and string orchestra. Donne's opening and closing line is:

Deigne at my hands this crowne of prayer and praise.

This was Colin's confident prayer to "the Power of the Unknown." I have never been more deeply moved by anyone's prayer.

✳ The Work We Do ✳

Today most of us are addicted to "stuff," a word that is either a verb or a noun. The verb means to fill up by packing things in. The noun refers to the things, activities, materials, achievements with which we fill our lives. Another, more sophisticated, term for "stuff" is "materialism" which is defined in the *Oxford English Dictionary* as "devotion to material needs or desires, to the neglect of spiritual matters; a way of life, opinion, or tendency based entirely upon material interests."

Our short-term economic goal is often to take full advantage of every opportunity for profit. With this attitude a long-term perspective on how we live our life is really not possible. E.F. Schumacher (1911-1977), a German-born British economist, tried to lead us off this fast track. In 1973 he published a book with the wonderful title *Small is Beautiful: Economics as if People Mattered.*[5] Schumacher starts with the understanding that people are more important than goods. If you stop to think about it, that idea would be revolutionary in today's workplace.

Three concepts jump out at me as I read Schumacher's book. First, work must give the human being a chance to develop her or his faculties. Second, our employment should enable each of us to overcome our preoccupation with self and join with others in a common task. Third, jointly we should bring forth goods and services for, as Schumacher puts it, a "becoming existence." I take that phrase to mean a graceful and harmonious life for all.

A number of my friends have opted out of better-paying jobs in order to work in environments where human values are paramount. Rebecca, who recently died at 49, was a schoolteacher who founded several schools. As each grew and became very successful, she would bid it goodby. She would then begin again because she did not want to lose contact with students. Wherever she was, true miracles in learning took place. Rebecca was one of the most respected teachers in her area. My neighbors, Basil and Barbara, founded a small family vineyard and winery in a remote area. Now, many years later, they are surrounded by some giants of the wine industry. They could have sold out for many times what they make each year. But they valued the lifestyle of a family working, and loving, their land. Another friend, Donald, is an internationally known businessman who has always avoided establishing a commercial empire. He has started quite a few telecommunication businesses. I have lost track of the number. He pioneers in some area, breaks through the traditional barriers, gets bought up by the "big boys," and starts over again, always with enthusiastic coworkers. Donald is also a bird-watcher, avid tennis player, and choral singer of J. S. Bach. I do not think any of these friends would see themselves as part of a "small is beautiful" movement. They are simply doing what to them makes sense, brings happiness, and helps the world in which they live.

Schumacher urges us, as part of our work, to plant a tree and look after it until it is established. In my experience, the type of work is not as important as the style of working. In 1955, I graduated from law school and entered the fray of professional life. A decade later, I was involved with nonprofit groups for improving the world in one way or another. I was probably planting more trees as a practicing attorney than as CEO of organizations concerned with the social good. In the world of agencies I discovered I was often relating to humanity in the abstract rather than to specific humans. When I later joined with others seeking a monastic life, I found more common encouragement to plant those trees. But had I really lived, in my twenties, "as if people mattered" I think I could have been a great tree planter while working in a school, a bookstore, a newspaper, an orchestra, or in any type of employment.

Mother Ann Lee (1736-1784), the foundress of the Shakers, preached:

Hands to work, hearts to God.

Following Mother Ann's advice may not always be easy. But it is worth the effort.

3

God and Paul Monette

No one can believe in everybody's God. Jews, Christians, and Muslims have to stretch to take in Native American creation stories. Buddhists have trouble with Christian concepts of a personal god. I do not want to believe in the God presented by fundamentalists of any religious persuasion, and they would not be satisfied with my understanding of God. We are all both believers and nonbelievers. And that is good.

"God" is a word for something absolute that is beyond our ability to express, conceptualize, or objectify. Whenever someone tries to ignore that mystery and presents the divine in a simplistic manner, doubt is not only understandable, it is necessary. Doubters can be prophets. My friend Paul Monette (1945-1995), may have been one of those.

Paul was a standard-bearer for the homosexual community and a gifted chronicler of the AIDS plague at the time I was writing memoirs about children and AIDS. An editor we both worked with introduced us. We took to each other right away, and soon discovered we had many common interests in addition to the AIDS pandemic. Paul was a poet and a man of vision. Our contacts were, for me, refreshing and challenging. He helped me to write and to laugh. In an inscription to a book, Paul wrote that our relationship gave him "respite from the battle." Our mutual fraternal regard was viewed with suspicion by Paul's more radical gay-rights associates and doubly so by some rigid traditionalists in the Catholic church. Both camps had trouble understanding that there was a spiritual dimension to Paul Monette, though to be fair, he did unequivocally proclaim himself an atheist.

Paul was raised a proper New England Episcopalian. But as a young adult, discovering his manhood and his sexuality, he wanted nothing to do with the image of God projected by organized religion. He was quite gentlemanly about his position that their God did not exist. There was no desire to be offensive. However, his denunciation of church authorities was a different matter.

For Paul, today's homosexuals are a tribe in the process of finding identity and strength. He took it very personally when his sexual orientation was denounced as unnatural in church documents or when an influential churchman objected to civil laws that protected gays and lesbians from discrimination. In Paul's writings, there are verbal pyrotechnics against church officials. "Minister of Hate" was how he described one cardinal—"The rabid dog in brocade . . . who laid down the law that loving gay was a matter of 'intrinsic evil.'"

Many religious people recognized Paul Monette as a deeply compassionate man courageously facing some of the profound spiritual issues of our age. I believe others discovered this in Paul before he was aware of it himself. Even then, as his partner Winston Wilde put it, "Paul kept his spirituality in the closet."

This is not the place to detail the struggles and victories of this remarkable man. Paul did that exceedingly well himself in his autobiographical books *Borrowed Time: an Aids Memoir; Becoming a Man: Half a Life Story* (which won a National Book Award for nonfiction) and *Last Watch of the Night: Essays Too Personal and Otherwise.*[6] What I want to relate here is the relationship of an atheist to his God. Because in this, as in many other areas, Paul Monette personified the quest and the quandary of a large number of people.

Paul died from AIDS at the age of forty-nine. My personal relationship with him had started seven years before. At first I tiptoed around any spiritual topics. Push the wrong button, I thought, and we have a big explosion. It was Paul himself who had to suggest that we forget about taboo areas in our relationship. It was only then I discovered Paul's well-known atheism was in reality a powerful defense of the first of the commandments given (Exodus 20:1-7) to Moses:

> I am Yahweh your God who brought you out of Egypt, where you lived as slaves. You shall have no other gods to rival me. You shall not make yourself a carved image or any likeness of anything in heaven above or on earth beneath or in the waters under the earth. You shall not bow down to them or serve them.

Paul was indeed an atheist, but, as he wrote, an atheist "by default." He would not accept the false gods created in the likeness of religious fundamentalists and used by them as tools to fashion the peculiar societies they advocated. The angry old man in the sky who conveniently denounces everything that is opposed by bigots is a false god created by bigots for the convenience of bigots. In refusing to accept these gods, Paul was, unknowingly, defending the God who refused to be rivaled.

Some influential twentieth-century theologians accepted that atheism could mean, for some people, a criticism of a particular image of God that was out of harmony with the age in which we lived. In reality, such an "atheist" was calling for a more authentic understanding of "God." In the last few weeks of his life, I discovered, much to my surprise, that Paul was one of the people of our age helping to define "God."

There were early clues that I had missed. Paul always talked about the "God of somebody." In *Last Watch of the Night,* Paul referred to a letter I wrote to him:

"Your brother, Toby," it was signed, and I saw it was the plain truth; we were a brotherhood of warriors. I didn't even flinch that Toby's God was in there somewhere. At least it wasn't the Pope's God.

Paul was a very decent person. In the Victorian era, there is no question he would have been called a "good Christian gentleman." In his final years, he preached to audiences in terms that were parallel to some concepts in the gospels. For example, at the State University of New York, where he accepted an honorary doctorate, he urged the students with considerable passion to "Lose your hate but not your rage. Go forth and heal the world!" I slowly began to understand that my friend was a good Christian gentleman in atheist drag.

We shared a love for Assisi, the city of St. Francis. The year before Paul died, we were both working on "Assisi chapters" for forthcoming works. This led to discussions of pilgrimages. Paul was a frequent pilgrim. More than once I was concerned about his failing health and would call him only to discover he had just made plans to take a cruise to the Baltic or some other new place. His last pilgrimage was to the little chapel of our spiritual community at Starcross, four months before he died. He had written in *Last Watch of the Night*: "So what is a pilgrimage anyway? I suppose it has to do with the baggage you carry and the baggage you manage to shed."

Part of the baggage we must manage to shed is other people's images of God. Shortly before his death, Paul called with some news. He had just given a sermon in a church-sponsored AIDS memorial service and was excited.

Toby, I surprised myself and shocked most of those in the pews.

What did you do?

I said when it comes right down to it, I need God as much as anyone else.

I had a great feeling of relief. It certainly was not a sense that my friend was "saved." It was joy that he had jumped over another barrier. Paul continued:

I told them the older I get the more I have come to realize that my atheism is a political stance against the religious fundamentalists. I think my position was needed and authentic, but there is more.

How did you talk about that "more"?

I defined "God" in terms of Paul Tillich's "ground of being." Don't you think it is good for them to think about that?

This was no deathbed conversion. Paul simply grew weary of the baggage of other people's images of the divine and cast them away. It is unfortunate that so many church officials handed out that baggage in the first place. Perhaps one of the great sins of church leaders has been in presenting a juvenile, shallow, and manipulative view of God to a world hungering for something more substantial. Like Paul, there are many who do not want the fundamentalist's God. They want God's God.

One of the most refreshing aspects of Paul was his plain and direct honesty. When he "came out of the trenches," as he put it, and focused attention on his spiritual life, Paul recognized the existential anxiety and alienation of our age and he longed for unity with a common ground of being. This was the quest that, according to Paul Tillich (1886-1965), gave each of us "the courage to be." There was never any doubt in my mind that Paul had found that courage long ago.

The troublesome question of "God" faces each of us. And, it does take courage to explore that question deeply throughout our lives. For people like Paul Monette, the statement "I can't believe in God" means an unwillingness to accept the shallow understandings of the divine. It is the beginning of a quest for the sacred, not the end of it.

❊ "When Heaven Is Open" ❊

Paul Monette experienced the loss of several men he loved and was facing his own death when he wrote:

> Grief is madness—ask anyone who's been there. They will tell you it abates with time, but that's a lie. What drowns you in the first year is a force of solitude and helplessness exactly equal in intensity to the love you had for the one who's gone.

He was right. We cannot adapt to textbook formulas for stages of grief that assume we are constantly evolving toward freedom from pain. We never get over the loss of someone we deeply love. Nor should we. But that is not the end of the story. There is a new life emerging. We can be, in fact we must be, born to a new life without the person for whom we grieve.

I will always be grateful to my friend Henri J. M. Nouwen (1932-1996), the spiritual writer, for pointing out an important process which often takes place in the months following a loss. Those gifts that we have prized most highly in someone who dies are often multiplied after death. Henri used the example of his own family. His father was loving but remote. His mother was the great letter writer, the one who tied the family together with emotional links. After her death, his father picked up her tasks. He became the one who tended to the emotional well-being of the family, wrote the letters, and became interested in the grandchildren's little victories and disasters. Other members of Henri's family did the same with one another. As a result, there was an increase in the emotional bonds within the family after his mother's death. Since Henri made this observation, I have found it in many situations. In regard to his much-loved partner, Roger, Paul Monette said in a interview with the TV journalist Charlie Rose, "In the eight years since his death, I have become Roger."

The death of one we love can increase the gifts that we so valued in that person's life. I have no doubt that the vitality of a person's spiritual life can and should continue after her or his death. That is one of the miracles of loss—and, there are others.

In 1987, when Josh, a little boy in our family, was dying, I first heard and used the phrase "heaven is open." I have since heard many people use similar words to describe a profound experience. As we stand beside someone who is dying, someone we love, the barrier between the cosmos and our individual experience fades. Our perceptions of existence change. I sometimes wonder if it is not similar to the experience we have at birth when we leave the cramped womb and emerge into the world. When "heaven is open" to the one we love who is leaving us, we who are staying behind are also truly open, perhaps for the first time. We will never be the same again. At these times, in the midst of the pain, we can gain a fresh vision of life which continues during a special year. The German poet Rainer Maria Rilke (1875-1926) wrote:

And you suddenly know: it was here!
You pull yourself together, and there
stands an irrevocable year
of anguish and vision and prayer.[7]

In German the last line of the poem is *Angst und Gestalt und Gebet*.

My adopted daughter Tina died from AIDS in 1991. She was almost three. Tina was a very special child. *Angst*, a dreadful feeling of deep anxiety, controlled my life after her death. Prayer, *Gebet*, helped bring more balance to my life. In time, the teeter-totter between pain and hope created a

kind of vision, the sense of a fundamental wholeness in my life, a *Gestalt*. In the pain and the grief
I encountered an ultimate point that I am comfortable calling "God."

4

The Stillpoint

The God-question for most adults is usually "Who is God?" or "What is God?" A child frequently asks "Where is God?"—a more productive question.

My quest for the divine often starts with a storm in my life. God is the calm eye for which I am searching. The symbol of "the stillpoint" is a spiritual interpretation of the process for making clay pots using a flat spinning wheel. Clay, it is said, must be thrown on the center of the wheel. If the potter attempts to fashion a vessel while the clay is on the side of the wheel, there is nothing but chaos. The force of the wheel works against the process. Even if the potter is very active, the result is a misshapen vessel at best. If the clay is on the center, the potter need apply no force. She simply positions her hands and the vessel is formed. She moves little. The power of the wheel is now working with her. It is true that the clay is spinning around, but there is a difference. At the very center of the wheel, there is a stillpoint. The vessel being shaped has its center over this point, and therefore it also contains a little unmoving point. The presence of this stillpoint allows the spinning sides of the vessel to be in harmony with the force of the wheel and the hands of the potter. All is well.

I have watched a few potters, and the process is not always as simple and neat as I have described, but it is a good image nonetheless. If I romanticize a bit, I can say that before I was born I lived at the stillpoint of my mother. I was at peace, even though I was aware of the chaos around me. In the same way, I would like to find the stillpoint of creation, our common mother, and to personally experience something of the fundamental mystery of existence. I am comfortable describing this desire as a quest for God. Now, how do I go about this search? There is a Zen tale I like because it gives me a vocabulary for two basic approaches in the spiritual life. This is what I remember of the story:

> Once Master Nan-in had a visitor, a restless student who wanted spiritual help and he wanted it now! The student's questions flowed without ceasing. Quietly the master offered tea. Even while holding the cup in his palm the student talked on about his concerns and desires. The master poured. The student talked. The tea filled the cup. Still the

student talked. Still the master poured. The hot tea over-flowed. "Hey," shouted the startled student, nursing his smarting hand, "can't you see this cup is full!" "Just so," said Nan-in, "and, like the cup, you are filled with your own ideas. How do you expect me to give you anything unless you offer me an empty cup?"

In my search for God I have usually come with a full cup, or at least half-full. If I look into the cup, I see the history of my quest, which reflects, in part, the evolution of God theories in my culture. This probably has much in common with every person's changing experience. For me, there has certainly been a continual unfolding of my understanding of God.

When I was a small child God was a myth, an explanation for things I did not understand. I only knew about humans, so God was a superhuman being who made things work. In my thoughts, God resembled my parents. I did not see my parents all the time, yet I knew they could control and fix most things. God was simply someone more powerful than my parents. Since God was a being, he/she had to live somewhere. I understood that God was to be found "up there." I was not sure where "up there" was, but I was confident God did not live in the same place I did.

As I matured, my concept of God slowly changed from superhuman to supernatural. God became a spiritual supreme being who lived, not "up there" but, everywhere at once. This brought God closer to me. But there was still a distance because my supernatural God functioned in an incorporeal realm that was fundamentally different from my physical surroundings. God lived "out there"—outside of my world. I could only meet this transcendent being fully at death. However, I felt this supernatural God had a personal interest in me. This was usually comforting, but not at those times when I was encouraged to think of God as a judge who was everywhere and knew all things. Add the dimensions of a future heaven or hell and God sometimes became frightening.

Either as a superhuman or a supernatural being, God is always functioning somewhere—"up there" or "out there." In my twenties, I had some trouble reconciling God's activities with what I was learning about science and people. It was easier to become an agnostic and pack God away with other mementos of childhood. I started thinking of God again when I was influenced by psychologists who focused attention on a divine element in human existence. I was impressed by the Swiss psychiatrist Carl Jung's (1875-1961) assertions that there was an unconscious depth in humankind through which we could experience the spiritual world. The God of religious psychologists lives not "up there" or "out there" but "in here." They sometimes speak of encountering an "other"—a wisdom, vague or very specific, which is a source of joy, fulfillment, and meaning in life.

I rested my quest "in here" for some time. Then I became interested in concepts of God that went beyond a single being, even one who resided "in here." I was fascinated by theologians who identified "God" with "being" itself. Paul Tillich, who I mentioned in the last chapter, explained God as the "ground of being." This continues to satisfy me, but I have to remember this is not the whole answer. Where, I often wonder, can I encounter that ground of being?

The quest for a transcendent God is one that strives to go beyond the commonplace and find a place of pure spiritual delight. "Transcendence" comes from a Latin word for raising oneself beyond ordinary human experience. "Immanence," whose Latin roots refer to remaining in, is often contrasted with "transcendence." And God can surely be found squarely in the middle of ordinary human experience.

My personal spiritual quest has turned toward an immanent or indwelling God coexisting with all of creation. If God is existence and each of us is a participant in existence, then God permeates the world and each of us. The experience of God becomes a very intimate phenomenon. But does this not negate the transcendent element? Has the familiar become too ordinary? "No," said Karl Rahner (1904-1984), the twentieth century's most prominent Catholic theologian. We each can encompass only a part of reality. The concept of God brings unity and sums up all reality. To understand God in this light will we not have to outgrow our idea of a personal God, one who is interested in each of us? Again, "No." Each of us is limited in our ability to become a person. God is that which is unlimited, the ultimate horizon of our perception of existence. Through encounter with God, we become more fully human. This view did not begin with Rahner. When addressing the men of Athens (Acts 17:23-31) Paul borrowed an expression from the poet Epimenides of Cnossos: ". . . he is not far from any of us, since it is in him that we live, and move, and exist." Many of us today are just beginning to explore what it really means to live, move, and exist in God. In order to do so, we must dump out these cups full of philosophies, theologies, psychologies, and ideas.

How do I actually experience the ground of being? I must find God on God's terms. The Chinese taught of "Wei Wu Wei"—action without striving. Chapter fifteen of the *Tao Te Ching* counsels:

Who can be still
  and let the muddy water slowly become clear?
Who can remain at rest
  and slowly come to life?

Who can remain still? Normally that does not include me. But from time to time I do truly rest and for those blessed moments, I do come to life.

I do not live always at the stillpoint, but when I have had the courage to present an empty cup, I have not been disappointed. On those fleeting occasions, I am unfettered by things, concepts, and ideas. There is nothing but a dimly perceived ultimate horizon, which I am satisfied to label "God." When I do not find a god created primarily out of my needs and desires, I catch a glimpse of God as God is, a mystery that cannot be contained in a corral of definitions.

The exploration of the sacred is interesting to me. It is also probably important to my understanding of existence. But I must always be careful. Much of what is in this chapter seems separated from how I actually attempt to be aware of the presence of God in my daily life. Is this chapter nothing but a cup full of sophisticated ideas and concepts? Certainly with an empty cup I could better appreciate that even my most cherished intellectual positions are crude attempts to put creation in a box. As I give up pondering the abstract nature of God, I discover an increased appetite to experience God in terms of what it means for me to become a more complete person.

Once, a young rabbinical student was complaining that he was unable to find the phrase "the face of God" in contemporary writings. "Why is that?" he demanded of his teacher. "Because," responded the old rabbi, "people don't look down as much as they once did."

Whenever I remember to look down, I usually do have a richer sense of the presence of God and the ultimate frontier of existence. Simplicity is always rewarding.

There are many paths to the stillpoint. No matter which way a person follows, we each become, little by little, more accepting of the divine element in our lives. The only important thing is that from time to time each one of us, who will all die, touch and become a part of that which will always be.

✳ Haiku Walks ✳

When my children were quite young, we started writing haiku poems together. We would more
or less follow the guidelines—seventeen syllables,
three lines, reflect the seasons, avoid the tempta-
tion to be clever. One day my young son was strug-
gling with the use of a pine tree in a haiku. I
remembered the great poet Bashō's (1644-1694)
advice, "If you want to know about the pine, go to
the pine tree!" And that is what we did.

My son's ideas about "pine" changed as he
pulled back the pine branches and stuck his face
near the trunk of a specific tree. This was the
beginning of our "haiku walks." We quietly strolled
outside looking for little moments that would be
the basis of a poem. It was rare that any of us actually wrote a poem. The walks became valuable
experiences in themselves, as if we were reading
the haiku in nature. We would begin by walking
quietly into the little garden or a meadow behind
the house. When one of us found something interesting he or she would, in very few words, point it
out. Almost always others added to the experience
by sharing how they saw the same thing in slightly
different ways.

It is exciting to go over familiar ground and find something unexpected. My children and I have seen, really seen, frosty spider webs reflecting the sunlight, the first squash blossom unfolding, plum petals dropping on an amazed cat, bees on the rosemary, tall trees going in and out of view in the mist, a little bird on a frozen woodpile, orange butterflies circling the chapel, and many, many ordinary things in an extraordinary way. We would come back from any haiku walk loaded with tales, and the occasional poem, to share with others. We also came back refreshed and more confident about living on this planet. The kids probably did not need that renewal and trust as much as I did.

Generations of Asian poets and painters have known the necessity of a refreshing place between our inner experience and the outer world. I have come to agree that grace and beauty are preconditions for my spiritual health. An ancient school of thought suggested that beauty had something to do with "harmony," a word whose Greek roots mean "fitting together."

There are countless ways of moving toward harmony. Each thought suggests several others: nature, gardening, cooking, watching the steam rise from a cup of tea or a funky corn dog, children, a home, looking at a pine cone, experiencing the seasons, poetry, art, music, walking, swimming, dancing, a ritual. What we experience is a balance between many things: what is known and what is unknown, the natural and the cultivated, the moving and the still. Out of such experiences come the healing and inspiration that is essential for our spiritual vitality.

We all need to sometimes transcend the sudden shocks that come along in life. Not long ago, I was to have a brief contact with an artist friend who was only days from death. I was not sure how to use that time. What were the important things I wanted to say or to hear? I went into the garden to think about it. We had recently planted some scruffy little plants. There were only a few leaves at the bottom and some flimsy stalks with tiny red flowers. I was looking at them with some disappointment when a hummingbird zoomed past me and connected with a red flower. It happened several times. As soon as one bird left another brightly colored one came. The thought occurred to me that we were not only growing little plants here, we were also growing hummingbirds! I realized that was what I really wanted to share with my friend who loved all living things. It turned out to be just the right thing to do. Since that time, I have often looked for the answer to a nagging question in a rose or a violet.

5

Friendly Metaphors

There are some wonderful images of God, but we must be careful as those images are created from our own individual experiences. This was the point of the Buddhist tale of the three blind men and the elephant. Each one defined the animal according to what he had encountered. The one, feeling the leg, declared the elephant a tree. When another's hands touched the trunk, it was obvious the elephant was a snake. The third man had run into the side and knew that the elephant was a wall. Each of us will define God by whatever partial experience we have had of the divine element in our life. It helps to know we are all spiritually blind. All of us. All.

God has never been seen. Paul wrote (1 Timothy 6:16) that his is a God "whom no one has seen and no one is able to see." We must really accept this fact about God. But it is not easy. Artists have filled walls, canvases, windows, books, and film with supposed likenesses. It is difficult to erase an image once it has been suggested. I heard Alan Watts (1915-1973), the Zen-Anglican philosopher and priest, challenge an audience with "you can have anything you want in life so long as you do NOT imagine an elephant in a bikini at any time within the next five minutes!" Nobody made it.

It is not too hard to discard the picture of the old man in a white robe sitting on a cloud. But it is also important not to take literally any other metaphor of God as a person—especially not as a male person. But it is almost impossible to eliminate all mental forms when contemplating God. Where does that leave us?

Some theologians, accepting that most of us will use metaphors of God, urge us to use more than one and to welcome tension between our images. They mean while it may be true, for example, that God is our father and/or mother, it is also true that God is not our father and/or mother. If we forget the "is not," we have created an idol to adore. We must leave room for the "is not" and be open to a constructive ambiguity. Entertaining more than one icon of God will sometimes keep our busy mind sufficiently occupied to let God sneak in somewhere.

I often find it helpful to concurrently keep active many different metaphors of the divine, some human and some not. I am not so interested in what God would look like, if God had a physical presence, as I am in how God would relate to me were we to meet in some physical dimension. In these imaginings, I have valued the delightful metaphors of people who dedicated their lives to living in the presence of the unseen God. In the fourteenth century, a number of these women and men referred to themselves as "Friends of God." There never was a formal institutional structure for them, but, at times, they did constitute a movement.

The Friends of God arose at a time when the world was crumbling. There was climatic deterioration producing a "little ice age" from 1315 to 1317. The result was a great famine. The lack of nutrition left many people weakened and contributed to the speed with which a plague, the "black death," spread across Europe in 1346. The plague rapidly reduced the population of the continent by one third. From 1317 to 1347, there were major struggles between the pope and the emperor that resulted in multiple civil wars. In addition, an unusual series of earthquakes and floods did great harm in many areas.

There is no doubt the Europeans of the fourteenth century had extraordinary emotional needs. The devastation made it difficult, at times, to remain sane. Many people felt God had either abandoned the people or was angrily taking revenge for their sins. The formalism of the religious institutions contributed to the perception of a great distance between God and humanity. Fierce and avenging images of God were described from the pulpits and depicted in religious art. Into this frightening abyss came people who shocked their contemporaries by referring to themselves as "Friends of God." These gentle folk, who claimed a direct experience of God, provided needed correctives to the common wrathful images of God.

The greatest concentration of the Friends of God was from Cologne down the Rhine to Basel and then continuing along the Rhine to Constance. This was also a major trade route. Strasbourg was a center for them. The movement was uniquely noted for not drawing distinctions between lay people and monks, nuns, or priests. They included people of all social ranks.

Were Friends of God merely denying the devastating realities of ordinary life? Were they escapists withdrawing into the interior life? I do not believe so. These were times of extreme crisis. The religious institutions' emphasis on exterior ritual was so lacking in spiritual nourishment that the phenomenon of the Friends of God was perceived by many at the time as a needed gift from Providence.

One of the last of the Friends of God was Nicholas von Flüe (March 21, 1417-March 21, 1487). He was an illiterate Alpine farmer with a remarkable wife and ten children. Nicholas had been a soldier, a state counselor, and a magistrate for the area of Obwalden in central Switzerland.

He considered himself a Friend of God for most of his life. In 1467 he left his family to join a community of the Friends of God in Strasbourg. He never made it there and eventually settled in a river gorge a few hundred yards from his family's farmhouse. In this wild and remote hermitage, Bruder [Brother] Klaus, as he was now known, served Switzerland as a statesman and peacemaker. Great and small sought him out for spiritual healing and political guidance. Today he is sometimes called the father of both the Swiss Confederation and the Swiss tradition of neutrality.

There are still daily pilgrimages to Bruder Klaus's hermitage. Pope John Paul II went there. So did I. While sitting alone in Bruder Klaus's cell and reflecting on his life, I had no doubt this man truly was one of God's friends.

Bruder Klaus had visions in which God appeared in forms quite contrary to the frightening popular images. In 1928 written reports of several of Bruder Klaus's visions were discovered in a monastic archive. They have been of great interest to a number of people, including Carl Jung.

In one of Bruder Klaus's visions, God is a singing pilgrim. A little local geography is necessary to understand the story. The farmhouse in which Bruder Klaus lived with his family is on a high hillside. Southeast is the gorge where he spent his last twenty years. Several valleys and smaller hills lie northwest of the farmhouse. Pleasant farms dot the landscape for many miles. Far in the distance rises massive Mt. Pilatus. It is actually a 7000-foot-high rock that is curiously named after Pontius Pilate, the Roman official who sentenced Jesus to death. Today there is a restaurant on top and cable cars going up and down. But in Bruder Klaus's day it was an ominous and mysterious presence. Beyond Pilatus is the major city of Lucerne. The mountain totally shields this urban area from view.

This vision begins with a pilgrim coming from the region "where the sun rises in summer." The pilgrim carries a staff and wears a cloak. He has a broad-brimmed hat on his head. As the pilgrim comes toward Bruder Klaus, he sings "Alleluia"—whereupon "everything between heaven and earth rang in harmony as small organ pipes are in tune with big ones." Bruder Klaus hears three perfect words, which are then shut away.

At the end of the song, the pilgrim asks Bruder Klaus for alms. Klaus is surprised to find he has a penny. The pilgrim takes off his hat and holds it out. Bruder Klaus gives him the penny and is amazed at how special it is to take alms in a hat. He stands before the pilgrim with excitement and joy and thinks him a truly beautiful man.

The pilgrim turns his dark eyes on Bruder Klaus and "many miracles took place." Mt. Pilatus sinks into the ground. Bruder Klaus can now see the whole world and he becomes aware of all the sins of the world. A great crowd of people appear. Behind the populace is the pilgrim, now called "The Truth." The people are facing in the opposite direction from the pilgrim and do not look at him. Each person has a large growth on the heart "as big as two fists." This growth is selfishness, which leads people astray so that they cannot bear to look at the pilgrim. Their response to the pilgrim is fear, abuse, and outrage. Bruder Klaus can see that the people are disappearing. In time, only the pilgrim remains.

The pilgrim's face changes into the face of Jesus. He is wearing a bearskin "with jacket and hose." The bearskin is flecked with gold and it suits him well.

Bruder Klaus knows the pilgrim is leaving and he asks where he is going. "Up to the country" is the only answer Bruder Klaus receives. The bearskin is now gleaming like well-polished armor.

The pilgrim is once again wearing a hat. He takes about four strides, turns, removes his hat, and bows. Bruder Klaus knows the pilgrim loves him greatly and it over-whelms Klaus. He feels he does not deserve the love. He also has a great love for the pilgrim in his own heart. Bruder Klaus sees that the pilgrim's face, eyes, and whole body are "as full of loving humility as a pot so filled with honey that it cannot hold another drop." Then, the pilgrim is gone.

Bruder Klaus is satisfied that the pilgrim has revealed to him everything he needs to know in heaven and on earth.[8]

The image of God as a singing pilgrim with a heart full of love is a truly nurturing concept. Bruder Klaus had other visions. Once he did behold God with a face of wrath, but the images were otherwise inviting and usually smiling. Bruder Klaus felt that God was reaching out to him in these visions—and with great courtesy and affection. The image of God was indeed that of a friend of humankind who constantly assured us that all was well between heaven and earth. This was a central theme of most of the mystics of this age. Julian of Norwich, the English mystic (1342?-1420?), described this divine contact with a few words which have been borrowed by many writers: "But all shall be well and all shall be well, and all manner [of] thing shall be well."[9]

Like Bruder Klaus, Julian was taught in her visions that the core of the Christian experience was to understand that each of us is loved, indeed, as she put it, "endlessly treasured" by God.

I feel comfortable in that tradition which accepts that there is some way of personally touching the creative mystery we label "God." To me the descriptions of this encounter used by Bruder Klaus, Julian of Norwich, and other mystics are as accurate as any other attempts, perhaps including the gospels.

In the end, all our efforts to define God with words are unsuccessful. However, it is possible to get more clarity on the life of Jesus of Nazareth, and that is important, as I hope the next chapter will show, for he is one of God's own attempts to help us understand and experience the sacred.

✳ Love and Spiritual Growth ✳

The Greeks had several words for love. *Eros* brought to mind erotic love in gods and in humans. The energy for *eros* was *libido*, the sexual drive. *Philia* meant affection and friendship. The love-word that was to mean the most to early Christians was *agape*, a love which unites us with God and each other. *Agape* is the term used in the New Testament to show the unlimited love God has for humanity and indeed to identify God as love itself (1 John 4:16): "God is love and anyone who lives in love lives in God, and God lives in him."

During the past few centuries, for most people in Western society, there has been more of an interest in *eros* than in *agape*. Religious professionals have not been very helpful here. Into this void came the psychologists who listened to the experience of their patients in order to understand love. Sigmund Freud (1856-1939) was among the first. Rollo May (1909-1994) asserted in *Love and Will* that Freud "struggled valiantly to reduce love to libido."[10] Sex is a natural aspect of many loving relationships, but it is not the whole story. In the mid-twentieth century, a growing number of psychologists considered love necessary for emotional health. They studied love despite the difficulties of defining and measuring it. Among these were May, Abraham Maslow (1908-1970)[11], and Carl Rogers (1902-1987). Once the door had been opened, many men and women explored the subject. Perhaps the public's interest peaked with M. Scott Peck's (1936-) very popular book *The Road less Traveled*. Peck was one of those who reestablished the connection between love and the spiritual. His definition of love was "the will to extend one's self for the purpose of nurturing one's own or another's spiritual growth."[12]

It is necessary to distinguish love from dependence, obsession, guilt, emotional desires, or the many forms of conditional love—I will love you if it makes me feel good, or if you will take care of me, or if you will let me control you, or if you will make me proud of you, or if this, or if that. Rogers defined love as the "unconditional positive regard"[13] for another person. That is, we transcend our self-centeredness to the extent that we have as much concern for another's welfare and growth as we have for our own. It also means having respect for and taking delight in the one we love. For most of us, understanding the nature of love in this sense is a process that slowly unfolds over a lifetime.

It starts with the child, but we cannot teach a child to love. What we can do is reassure our children that they are loved. Words are not enough. It has to do with sharing ourselves, our time, and our values. They must feel secure, but overprotection is not love. Native Americans had a wonderful idea with the cradle boards that enabled a mother to carry her baby back-to-back. Even the youngest child felt the warmth of her mother while looking out at the world and became comfortable with it. It is in such settings that a child develops joyful relationships with birds and flowers, breezes and clouds. This is the beginning of feeling at home in the universe.

In adolescence, love and infatuation get all mixed up with each other. The awakening of the sexual side of our nature is a powerful and confusing event. No one I know has ever glided smoothly through puberty. It is not an easy time, and choices will sometimes be made that are later regretted. When a young person asks for my advice, I sound rather old-fashioned. I would like to see them less casual about moving from friendship (*philia*) to sexual pleasure (*eros*). I hate to see childhood cut short by very early sexual activity. I think they are happier in the long run when sex is connected to more mature loving relationships (*agape*). But it does not matter much what I think. A young person has to sort this all out within her or his own experience, options, and values. I have great confidence in the ability of our youth to work things out. They certainly do better than I did at their age.

Love, that "unconditional positive regard," has to be present for an emotionally and spiritually satisfying adult relationship. Where it is present, there is a refreshing spontaneity and simplicity. The partners value their delight in thoroughly enjoying each other. Although they may not use these words, they see God in each other and in their life together.

The initial romance and passion of a marriage will fade. But there is a great difference between an intimate partnership where husband and wife care for each other and a loveless non-union. There is an obligation in marriage to develop healthy relationships between the spouses. If that cannot or does not happen then divorce may be, and I select the word carefully, necessary. There are times when a marriage is destructive to the partners and the children. Such unions should end and many religious traditions have recognized that necessity.

When Jesus spoke against divorce, he was trying to protect women. At that time a man could divorce his wife but not the other way around. Divorce meant the woman was cast out of her family with few options. It is really twisting Jesus' compassionate concern to make it appear that the absolute indissolubility of marriage is a divine law. It is also unreasonable to offer only the option of single life to those whose marriages have failed, often at an early stage. Most people have the need of intimate loving relationships. There are also the needs of children and issues of justice, especially when the party wishing to remarry has been abandoned against her or his will. To me, the greatest concern should be for the flowering of love. If a wrong turn was taken the first time and there is a second chance for two people, and perhaps children, to experience the grace of a good marriage, I think it is presumptuous to stand in the way.

Gay and lesbian couples today have the same spectrum of loving relationships as do heterosexual couples, and the same grace to find happiness. The attitudes of society have changed quite a bit toward homosexuals. A big factor is the growing clarity, that for gays and lesbians, as even the U.S. Catholic bishops expressed it in 1997, "homosexual orientation is experienced as a given, not as something freely chosen." Some religious people are concerned about the prohibitions against homosexuality found in the Bible (Genesis 19:4-11; Leviticus 18:2; 20:13; Romans 1:24-27; 1 Corinthians 6:9-10; and 1 Timothy 1:9-10). It is certainly the case that heterosexual relations are the assumed biblical norm. But the scriptural warnings against homosexuality are much more concerned with idolatry (homosexual prostitution was found in many temples of alien gods), the violation of hospitality, or the abuse of children than basic sexual orientation.

There are many words written in praise of young love, but not many about old love. It is important to know there is a patina to love. The relationship between people who have been together can grow deeply beautiful with age. After so many years together, the difference between "I" and "Thou" has begun to blur, as has the difference between sex and a sunset, a prayer and putting wood in the stove, God and a cup of tea. Old love can be very rich when the sensual and the spiritual come together. There may sometimes be sorrow in looking back and seeing how self-centered one has been but also a joy from finally beginning to understand what happiness is all about. Old love is a unique appreciation of the divine spark in all the life around us. Figures of an elderly couple are a part of many Christmas crib scenes in Provence. The legend is that they have come to the Christ-child with a request—to die on the same day. The older I get, the better I understand that tale.

The God of creation intended us to be fulfilled in intimate relationships. Every woman and man will face different challenges and have different outlooks on love. However, there is one proverb we should all agree upon and remember,

Where there is love, there also is God.

6

Jesus the Brother

esus of Nazareth is a bridge between the divine and the
human, but many people are tired of hearing about Jesus.
The American author Walker Percy (1916-1990) observed
that the Christian novelist was like a person "who has found
a treasure hidden in the attic of an old house but he is writing for people who have moved out to the suburbs and who
are bloody sick of the old house and everything in it."[4] Percy
was concerned about the despair born of the rootlessness of
people in contemporary society. He wanted us to get up in
that attic and rediscover our treasures. That means we have
to ignore a lot of shallow references to Jesus in the media
and in pulpits.

In each generation, the greatest obstacle to a person
becoming a follower of Jesus has been encountering self-
righteous Christians. It is helpful to remember that Jesus

himself was not a Christian. He was an unschooled Jewish layman who ignored established religious traditions and institutions. The "good news" he brought was that everyone can have hope because human well-being is the keystone in God's plan of salvation, and that plan is universal. It includes everyone. How is the plan realized? If we transcend our fears and our self-interest, we can together make the kingdom of God a reality on earth.

The author of these beatitudes (Matthew 5:3-10) was a gentle and quiet person:

How blessed are the poor in spirit:
> the kingdom of Heaven is theirs.

Blessed are the gentle:
> they shall have the earth as inheritance.

Blessed are those who mourn:
> they shall be comforted.

Blessed are those who hunger and thirst for righteousness:
> they shall have their fill.

Blessed are the merciful:
> they shall have mercy shown them.

Blessed are the pure in heart:
> they shall see God.

Blessed are the peacemakers:
> they shall be recognized as children of God.

Blessed are those who are persecuted in the cause of uprightness:
> the kingdom of Heaven is theirs.

It was a chaotic world into which Jesus was born. Common people simply tried to exist between the clashing of the various political and religious leaders. The ranks of the poor were increasing. A growing number of people were compromising with the Roman conquerors in order to gain a livelihood. These pragmatists were ostracized from Jewish religious fellowship.

Jesus grew up among rural people in Galilee. He lived in a village near a large urban center where many different cultures mixed. Galilee was important for trade and social thought. Nonetheless, the cosmopolitan citizens of Jerusalem considered the people of Galilee unsophisticated and uneducated. Even the Galilee accent was a cause for ridicule. Endless debates raged in Jerusalem over complicated religious issues. By contrast, the Jew of Galilee was concerned with the basic questions of living.

Jesus worked with his hands and relaxed with his friends to whom he taught a way of moving through life, of practicing the art of living, which brought hope. He gave himself to all people, including the outcast, the poor, and the suffering. Jesus did not encourage his friends to renounce their humanity but to fulfill it. He rejected religious laws when they stood in the way of human happiness. "The Sabbath was made for people, not people for the Sabbath" he is quoted as saying (Mark 2:27) in a phrase borrowed from the Jewish sage Hillel (30 B.C.-A.D. 9).

Jesus addressed the pains of the people, but he did not fit into any of the acceptable classifications for religious leaders in his day. He was not a priest as were the leaders of the religious establishment, nor was he a revolutionary like the Zealots. Unlike the Essenes, he did not withdraw from society. The Pharisees did not recognize him as a scholar schooled in the intricacies of the moral law.

It is not surprising that Jesus was accused by religious leaders of many transgressions: breaking the Sabbath; promising salvation and forgiving sins; casting out devils with the help of the devil; setting himself above the established authorities, indeed setting himself above Moses; eating and drinking with sinners; and, perhaps most seriously, calling God his father. The God of Jesus became a loving parent, not a stern monarch. He described God with the informal word "Abba," meaning "Dad." This familiarity shocked many of his contemporaries, while it brought joy to others.

Jesus was a spiritual oddball who provoked both religious and civil leaders, and eventually he was executed because of that. To the Roman official, Pontius Pilate, Jesus was a threat to good order, and Pilate eliminated Jesus just as he had many other irritating people.

At the cross Jesus placed an ultimate trust in God. His remarkable presence was experienced after the crucifixion, and the faith and history of the Christian communities began.

This man from Galilee was, and is, one of those beings who provide a link between the stillpoint of God and the ordinary life of human existence. His followers labeled him with the Greek *Christos* meaning "the anointed one." It is the equivalent of the Hebrew "messiah." What was the relationship of the human Jesus and the divinely anointed "Christ"?

In Mahayana Buddhism, there are "bodhisattvas," holy people who postpone complete individual enlightenment while they help all the rest of us awaken spiritually. By contrast, the Hindu awaiting the tenth earthly incarnation of Vishnu, the god who preserves us, has a different perspective. It might be said, crudely, that bodhisattvas are humans who have become divine and are helping all of us in a related process. Vishnu, on the other hand, is a god become human. He is a fully divine being manifesting himself in various human forms. Which was Jesus?

The Gospel of John presents Jesus as a God who became a human. I have never been comfortable with the concept that Jesus was a preexisting, eternal divinity who came to earth and masqueraded as a mortal. I prefer the portraits in the Gospels of Matthew, Mark, and Luke where Jesus comes through as a fully human being who wandered throughout the secular world and challenged existing religious concepts.

Before the term "Christian" was accepted by Jesus' friends, they described themselves simply as "brethren" or "disciples," which comes from a Greek word for "learner." What were they learning? It was a certain style of living sometimes called "The Way" (Acts 19:23). They had a concern for the practice and style of living introduced by Jesus. His followers were occasionally known as "people of the Way."

The Old Testament, as we now organize it, is made up of the law, the historical books, the wisdom books, and the works of the prophets. Wisdom literature celebrates human experience. With the five wisdom books (Job, Proverbs, Ecclesiastes, Ecclesiasticus, and Wisdom) is also grouped the Song of Songs and the Psalms. All these writings present suggestions for a fulfilling lifestyle with little reference to religious doctrine, and are influenced by the literature of neighboring cultures. The uniqueness of the sages of Israel is that these concerns for the practical life of an individual are presented as if they are part of God's plan.

Jesus was a sage of the wisdom tradition, for it was in this area that he uniquely restored balance and wholeness. One of Jesus' most powerful means of teaching was a dynamic personal contact that challenged the disciple to a radical conversion of life. There was a piercing touching of the heart that cut through many preoccupying problems and mental concepts. The memory of Jesus is vividly set forth in parables, often troubling stories and similes whose relevance was not always obvious. The parable explains, but it cannot be explained.

How do we approach a parable? We cannot defuse it with our rational powers, but we can learn from it with our intuitive gifts. The process has something to do with the recognition of a personal challenge that affects us at a deep level and calls forth some kind of individual response. A parable of children is found in both Matthew and Luke (Matthew 11:16-19, Luke 7:31-35). The more complete Luke version reads:

> What description, then, can I find for the people of this generation? What are they like? They are like children shouting to one another while they sit in the market place:

> "We played the pipes for you,
> and you wouldn't dance;
> we sang dirges,
> and you wouldn't cry."

> For John the Baptist comes, not eating bread, not drinking wine, and you say, "He is possessed." The Son of Man [Jesus] comes, eating and drinking, and you say, "Look, a glutton and a drunkard, a friend of tax collectors and sinners." Yet Wisdom has been proved right by all her children.

On the rational level, the parable of the children is used to describe the differences between John the Baptist, who emphasized repentance of sin, and Jesus, who offered a joyful fellowship. But that is not the deep import of the message. Jesus is speaking to each of his listeners by use of a poignant song. We were presented with two options. We have failed to respond to either. The dirges of John did not call forth our tears. We did not dance to the pipes of Jesus. What then will awaken us to our spiritual hunger?

Another disturbing twist in the parable is that the children themselves, those who most yearn to play, are chanting this song back and forth. We are like hungry people throwing bread to each other without ever tasting it. Everything has been presented that it is possible to present, and we, the children, will not respond. A deep communication is contained in the parable's haunting song. Is this a cosmic lament lasting two thousand years? When will we dance? When will we cry? These are ageless questions and they relate to Walker Percy's and many other writers' concern for despair in the spiritual life.

Our failure to respond to God's songs distances us from God. For his friends, Jesus was a being who reduced the distance between what is human and what is divine. In the next chapter we take up the story of someone Jesus helped—a short man who, like many of us, was having trouble seeing Jesus.

7

The Man in the Sycamore Tree

Who was Jesus? Most of us turn to the gospels for an answer. I am fond of Luke's gospel, which was probably written about A.D. 85-90. None of the gospels are biographies. They are attempts to bring Jesus' message to particular communities, each with differing attitudes and needs. The Gospels of Mark and Matthew were written for Christian communities withdrawn from society on the assumption that Jesus would soon reappear and the world would cease to exist. By contrast, Luke addressed people who assumed they would live out their lives within the Roman Empire.

Luke was not writing as a historian. He was attempting to put the story of Jesus into a context of issues relevant primarily to some non-Jews known as "God-fearers." These Greeks and Romans were attracted to the monotheistic faith and ethical standards of Israel. Many of them were fascinated by what they heard of Jesus but troubled by the fact that the people of Israel seemed to have rejected him. Luke wanted to show that followers of Jesus posed no threat to good order and were reasonable and ethical people. More than in the other gospels, Luke's image of Jesus portrays a humanistic savior interested in the poor, the oppressed, and the outcast. Luke's is also a gospel of prayer. It is not enough to wait for a second coming. We are encouraged to encounter the divine in daily life.

There is an optimistic and joyful tone to Luke. The gospel ends with, "They worshiped him and then went back to Jerusalem full of joy; and they were continually in the Temple praising God" (24:52-53).

This is in strong contrast to the probable original ending of Mark, ". . . and they said nothing to a soul, for they were afraid . . ." (16:8).

A big stumbling block for Luke's sophisticated audience was the peculiarity of following after an executed criminal. Luke portrays Jesus as a good man destroyed not by the Jewish people but by corrupt and evil political authorities responding to fears and prejudices. The civilized world was familiar with a similar situation when the wise, just, and pious Socrates (470 B.C.-399 B.C.) was indicted for "impiety" because of his corruption of the young and his neglect of the religious traditions. Luke presents the innocent Jesus as a Socrates and emphasizes the nobleness of the death. For example, Matthew (27:54) and Mark(15:39) have a Roman centurion announce at the moment of Jesus' death, "In truth this man was a son of God." But in Luke the centurion "gave praise to God" and proclaimed the more Hellenistic accolade, "This was a great and good man" (24:47).

The well-educated Luke has a broader social attitude than is found in the other gospels. Women are portrayed as having a more significant role in the ministry of Jesus. He advocates a prudent and proper use of material resources rather than a rejection of all earthly goods. Addressing a non-Jewish community with no particular historical concern for the poor, Luke emphasizes the need for charity.

As is true in all the gospels, Luke demonstrates that Jesus brings hope for all who are alert and willing to seize the unique opportunity of an encounter with him. There are several Greek words for time. The most common is *chronos*, the regular, measured beat of the clock. But the word for time more frequently used in the gospels is *kairos*, which connotes a moment of decision and change, an instant pregnant with opportunity.

An essential characteristic of the encounter with Luke's Jesus was that a person found herself or himself in a process of discovery. It was as if some latent vitality in the soul were liberated. The experience of Jesus gives an individual's life a new meaning. Luke demonstrates this in the story of an unpopular fellow named Zacchaeus (19:1-10).

[Jesus] entered Jericho and was going through the town when a man whose name was Zacchaeus made his appearance; he was one of the senior tax collectors and a wealthy man. He was anxious to see what kind of man Jesus was, but he was too short and could not see him for the crowd; so he ran ahead and climbed a sycamore tree to catch a glimpse of Jesus who was to pass that way. When Jesus reached the spot he looked up and spoke to him: "Zacchaeus, come down. Hurry, because I must stay at your house today." And he hurried down and welcomed him joyfully. They all complained when they saw what was happening. "He has gone to stay at a sinner's house," they said. But Zacchaeus stood his ground and said to the Lord, "Look, sir, I am going to give half my property to the poor, and if I have cheated anybody I will pay him back four times the amount." And Jesus said to him, "Today salvation has come to this house, because this man too is a son of Abraham; for the Son of Man has come to seek out and save what was lost."

The historicity of this story can be questioned because it appears only in Luke's gospel. However, it resembles many other gospel stories and presents a probable composite of such encounters.

Jesus was a friend of all humanity. Nowhere would Jesus'

friendliness be more tested than with Zacchaeus and his fellow tax collectors. They were thoroughly despised by the Jews and with good reason. The tax collectors profited from serving the Roman oppressor. They collected all the annoying minor taxes on goods coming to market, including salt and other common articles. These duties were in addition to heavy taxes the Jews paid to support whatever government was controlling them at the time. Imperial direct taxes on land amounted to about 20 percent of the value of the crops produced on the land and separate per capita taxes were levied on a person's wealth. Rome also authorized the religious authorities to collect assessments. Much more burdensome than the relatively small annual Temple tax were the tithes by which God as owner of the earth was to be repaid by a portion of the "first fruits" of the people's labor. These tithes were used to support the large priestly class.

The Jews were almost taxed out of existence by Roman and Temple authorities. It is no wonder they despised the Jewish opportunists who arrogantly examined the goods of all and exacted additional duties at every city gate and crossroad. These grasping exploiters had made a contract with a Roman official to pay an annual fixed sum in exchange for rather broad authority to reimburse themselves through collecting indirect duties. There was much dishonesty in the system.

The tax collector and his family formed a separate caste. When one member of a family became a tax collector, the entire family became social outcasts. They were sinners who were grouped, by Jewish leaders, with "harlots" and "heathens." Yet Jesus held out the hand of friendship even to this despised group. Why? Perhaps to show there was no limit to God's love. One of the twelve apostles, Matthew (also known as "Levi") was a tax collector.

By the time of Jesus, most tax collectors had not personally made the choice to follow that occupation. They had been born into the alienated social class. No matter how despicable their activities, they were pursuing one of the few lifestyles open to them. Jesus gave them an alternative, and people like Matthew and Zacchaeus responded. This was in contrast to the more respectable members of the religious and social establishment who generally did not respond to Jesus' invitation.

Proper people found Jesus an irritant. He offered freedom in exchange for the sacrifice of privilege. The public sinner often responded happily; the righteous leader of society seldom made the exchange.

Zacchaeus' encounter takes place just before Jesus begins his fatal Jerusalem ministry. It is Luke's summing up of the good news preached on the journey to Jerusalem. The setting is Jericho, arguably the oldest city in the world, but nonetheless a place associated with new beginnings.

There Joshua, centuries before, had led the chosen people into the promised land. Near there Jesus had received his own baptism and perhaps first became aware of the unique possibilities of his existence. Three gospels relate the healing of a blind man in Jericho (Matthew 20:29-34, Mark 10:46-52, Luke 18:35-43). It is a place for new direction, vision, and hope.

Luke gives Senior Tax Collector Zacchaeus some individuality. Like the blind man, Zacchaeus wants to see. He is too short, so he climbs a tree. He asserts himself to see a man who represents something Zacchaeus values in his innermost heart. The name "Zacchaeus" means "pure." There is a spot of purity in all of us, no matter how corrupt we may have been.

Something is beginning to bubble up inside of Zacchaeus. He is stretching out, even to climbing up a tree. This tree, the sycamore, is related to the fig, but its fruit is almost inedible. However, the sycamore is not useless; it gives refreshing shade. Like Zacchaeus, the outcast, the sycamore also has a use in the scheme of things.

The exchange between Jesus and Zacchaeus is playful. A short man scurries up a tree with no concern for his dignity. Ignoring all the crowds and the monumental events taking shape, Jesus responds to this one individual and gives him more than he asks for. "I must stay at your house today." Matching Zacchaeus' enthusiasm, Jesus has called out in a most friendly fashion. Miraculously, he even uses Zacchaeus' name. There are two reactions. Zacchaeus "hurried down and welcomed him joyfully," but the self-righteous citizens complained, "He is going to stay at a sinner's house." It is not for Jesus to prove his faith in Zacchaeus. Instead, Zacchaeus demonstrates the results of this encounter with Jesus: "I am going to give half my property to the poor." Who among the critics had the courage to match this loving outpouring?

Zacchaeus did not give all his wealth away. He agreed to what was just, to pay back four times to any person he may have cheated. But otherwise he was giving away, in effect, his surplus, that which gave him a privilege above others. This is consistent with Luke's account, in the Acts of the Apostles, of disciples selling their goods and possessions and sharing the proceeds. They probably did not dispose of houses they lived in nor goods they used. They sold the houses they rented out and their surplus goods. Luke presents a realistic view of wealth to his practical readers. The poor could be helped with what was not needed by those better off. The material aspects of the kingdom of God come about simply by the wealthy taking their surplus and giving it to those in need.

Zacchaeus transcended the corrupting influences of his past. The complex had become simple again.

Today salvation has come to this house, because this man too is a son of Abraham.

"Salvation" is not a popular word. It is too often on the lips of the self-righteous and the narrow-minded. But it is a good word deriving from roots which meant "entire," "whole," "wholesome." As with Zacchaeus, salvation will come to our house if we value becoming more whole and wholesome.

✳ A Dance of Life ✳

The way in which a person, and a society, lives a wholesome and happy life is an ongoing quest. I think God left it largely to each generation to figure it all out for its time. It is reasonable to look to our religious traditions, but there is often a problem about how this wisdom is presented to us. If it is overly harsh and rigid, it is ineffective and counterproductive. Rather than dogmas, we need to learn the steps in a dance of life that can be used in meeting difficult situations.

The Flemish Catholic scholar, Edward Schillebeeckx (1914-) sees no essential new doctrine or religious teaching stemming from Jesus. Schillebeeckx maintains Jesus proclaimed the kingdom of God by putting the "good news" into practice. It is this "right practice," to borrow a Buddhist term, we are invited to follow. Schillebeeckx closed his book *Jesus: An Experiment in Christology* with a story from the Jewish philosopher Martin Buber (1878-1965). A rabbi's grandfather was paralyzed. One day the grandfather was asked to say something about his own spiritual teacher. The grandfather tried to explain how the saintly man would leap and dance about while at prayer. But it was not possible to describe in words how this was done. Soon the grandfather was demonstrating the dance and his paralysis was cured.[15]

Spiritual stories cannot be transmitted unless they are lived out. To know the way of Jesus, and to seek a cure of our own spiritual paralysis, we must dance the dance of Jesus. How? The starting point has to do with the realities of life in our age. Some recurring themes today harm both individual and community life. There are different opinions on what all these issues are, but most lists would include a reference to the growing selfishness and the resulting loneliness. Does the experience of the followers of Jesus have anything to contribute to that issue? Yes. The same could be said of the followers of Buddha, Muhammad, or any other religious leader. They are all needed for there is an urgent necessity to encourage the development of a global ethical perspective—a common ground for how we relate to each other. One of the most important things the followers of Jesus could offer in this process is the gentle, yet challenging, approach of Jesus. As was mentioned in chapter 6, this style and practice of life was sometimes simply called "The Way" (Acts 19:23).

Chinese sages would have labeled this concern for "The Way" as "Tao."

Part of Jesus' way was to serve as a host at meals for those who, for various reasons, were not welcome at most respectable tables. Eating and drinking with his friends and social outcasts was a very inclusive style of life. Jesus encouraged people and made them happy. Like ourselves, Jesus was in a process of realizing the potential of his personhood, which included merging the divine and the human potential. In a more limited but nonetheless deeply significant way, each of us has been invited to merge those same elements in ourselves.

Much of what Jesus' companions learned must have come from observing his style of coping with ordinary life. They were always walking somewhere with him. The little things that happened on those journeys would have had a profound impact on them. How did he travel down the road? How did he approach the necessities of food and shelter? What was his response to ordinary misfortunes? Most important, how did he act toward others in the small moments of these long trips? The German theologian and pastor, Dietrich Bonhoeffer (1904-1945) gave us a clue when he referred to Jesus as a "man for others."[16] Jesus has made a deep impression on history. His style of living, his Tao, presupposes so intimate an identity with existence itself that we can only term it "love."

If I can be a person for others and find God in others as well as in myself, then I can dance around the universe with another human being. It is a relationship I cannot control. I am vulnerable, and perhaps afraid, as I encounter someone who is encountering me. However, as a result, I lose my separateness and become more fully human. It is the most nourishing and authentic encounter I can have with another person—and also with God.

THE PRESENCE OF THE SACRED

8

Sacred Experience

How do we become aware of the presence of the sacred in our lives? What are the tools with which we can refresh our faith as we move through the challenges of everyday life? It was perhaps less difficult for our primitive ancestors who experienced the whole natural world as a sacred reality. The rational, the practical, the psychological, and the spiritual aspects of life were all integrated, and they were all sacred. The quest for the sacred has continued to be a part of the way in which many, perhaps most, women and men have unfolded the wonder of their humanity.

An awareness of the sacred in ordinary life distinguished early Christian communities from people primarily concerned about either the secular or the occult. Following their Jewish heritage, the first Christians understood that baking bread for a gathering of the brothers and sisters, collecting herbs to relieve the pains of the sick, and watering a garden were all tasks that naturally led them to a cognizance of the divine.

In the Middle Ages, people continued to assume that God was very active in their lives. Francis of Assisi (1181/82-1226), and others like him, found God everywhere:

> Praised be you, my Lord, for all your creatures, especially for Brother Sun, who brings us the day and gives us light. He is beautiful and shines with a great splendor, reminding us of you.
>
> Praised be you, my Lord, for Sister Moon and the stars, in heaven. You formed them clear and precious and beautiful.
>
> Praised be you, my Lord, for Brother Wind, and for the air, cloudy and serene, and every kind of weather by which you give sustenance to your creatures.
>
> Praised be you, my Lord, for Sister Water, which is very useful and humble and precious and chaste.
>
> Praised be you, my Lord, for Brother Fire, through whom you light the night. He is beautiful and playful and robust and strong.
>
> Praised be you, my Lord, for our Sister Mother Earth, who sustains and governs us, and who produces varied fruits with colored flowers and herbs. . . .
>
> Praised be you, my Lord, for our Sister Bodily Death, from whom no living person can escape.

At the same time as Francis was singing to the God he found everywhere, medieval churchmen were working to systematize and institutionalize our response to divine love. The result of their efforts was an increasing emphasis on seven official sacred acts or "sacraments," all of which normally required the services of an ordained cleric.

All faiths acknowledge milestones in the journey of life: birth, maturity, partnership, death. In the medieval Christian world, this acknowledgment was conveyed through the seven sacraments. In baptism the infant was claimed for God. Penance let the sinner be reconciled with God. The young person was strengthened in confirmation. Matrimony or holy orders sanctified a vocation. Anointing helped the afflicted transcend sickness and pain, especially in the face of death. The Eucharist was a means for a group to gather, giving praise and thanks to God. At the Eucharist, or "Mass," the community is nourished in the same way Jesus gave of himself to his disciples on the night before he was condemned to die.

The seven sacraments are a neat and systematic way of viewing sacred reality. But manifestations of the divine in time and in space cannot be confined forever in a medieval theological box. Today, as in the early days of Christianity, people find the presence of God in all aspects of life.

There are many ways in which I have experienced sacred reality. I find it in the silences and in thoughts and words I sometimes label "prayer" and "meditation." I also find that same reality in nature, history, and in the cycles and changes of life, years, and days. Increasingly, I am learning to recognize the sacred in people. There is a sacrament of people. In the chapters that follow, I will share some experiences in these spheres. They are experiences that I believe have been common in many spiritual traditions.

9

Sacred Hours

On a warm October day, I was sitting in our orchard with Paul Monette, who had come up from Los Angeles. It was late in the afternoon. The fading light filtered through the red, yellow, and brown leaves of the fruit trees. Paul was frail and partially blind. He would die in four months. The conversation turned to things he could still eat and enjoy. He mentioned apples with some longing in his voice. I got up and walked to a nearby tree that still had some fruit. Paul was amazed when I put a large yellow apple before him. There was a long silence as he stared at the apple. Paul then spoke of the homes of his boyhood in New England. "I had forgotten," he mused, "that every family had a fruit tree. That makes a difference in how you live."

Sometimes we forget about when the world moved at a simpler and more predictable pace. Change, and especially the accelerating rate of change, presents each generation with unique spiritual challenges. Human history can be viewed as a success story of dominating the environment. But every accomplishment has been accompanied by some loss.

Half a million years ago, we learned how to manage fire. With this wonder, we pushed back darkness and modified the severity of the seasons. With fire we could drive animals out of caves, harden spears, and cook. Around these primitive hearths, our first sense of community began and with it the development of language. All of this seems like wonderful progress. But, as we learn in a Greek myth, it is also a violation of the natural order and there are consequences. Prometheus stole the fire for us and as a result, according to one legend, Pandora was sent to punish us. All manner of evil, hard work, and disease flew out of her great jar. All that remained in it was hope.

Homo sapiens branched off the trunk of our ancestral tree at least 250,000 years ago. It took 210,000 years more for us to reach our present physical state. As the millennia passed, we learned to live closer together and to share our memories and experiences. About 10,000 years ago, we had evolved from hunting and gathering to agriculture. That progression took about 30,000 years. The results were startling. Where thousands of acres had been needed to support a family, now 25 was enough. This led to a greatly increased population. We established villages, and civilization, as we define it today, gradually evolved. Farming and the domestication of animals produced an economic surplus that supported great cities where many talents developed, including writing and literature. Recorded history had begun. It had taken us 500,000 years to reach that point. Since then, the rate of change has been continually accelerating.

The problem of rapid change did not fully surface until the twentieth century. It became apparent in the 1960s that the biggest psychological (some said "psycho-spiritual") problem of our age would be the ability to adapt to the increasing rate of change.

When I was born in 1931, families in our area of rural Mississippi were being introduced to electricity. My parents saw changes that were, in some ways, similar to what our ancestors experienced with fire 500,000 years ago. The difference was that it took thousands of years to absorb the changes brought about by fire, whereas my parents had to adapt to major changes within only a few years. Why the difference? It has something to do with population and education, or at least shared learning. The rate of change is a communal process. In the very sparsely populated prehistoric times, a person could utilize only a few other reserves of memories and experience. In the 1930s, millions of people were able to build on each other's memories and experiences.

A person born in the 1980s has benefited from almost unlimited experiences and would consider the rate of change in the 1930s incredibly slow. Young people have absorbed the influence of television, jet travel, the computer, interactive dialogue, the Internet, and many other new and wonderful examples of progress. But, just as with Prometheus' gift of fire, there are consequences to each new development. We are drifting farther and farther away from the time when the fruit tree in the backyard kept us anchored to nature.

The word "liturgy," now only associated with religious rites, originally meant any public service. Frequently that service was to protect our psyche from being damaged in the accelerating pace of social change by providing links with a simpler past. We need to have ways to draw nourishment from a cycle of life more fundamental than the patterns of existence we have managed to artificially construct.

When the sky is changing at dawn or at dusk I am often aware of the presence of God. Many people have the same experience. When a whole community attempts to respond to this awareness, liturgical cycles are born. Some relate to the seasons of the year, others to the stages of individual human life. Jewish tradition was the major influence on Christian liturgy. The seven-day week was the basic unit. The high point of the week was the Sabbath meal in the home, which followed the reading of scripture in the synagogue. Christians changed the day to Sunday but imitated the Jewish rituals in the two major sections of the Mass or Eucharist. The synagogue readings became the "Liturgy of the Word." The Sabbath meal, which was the format for Jesus' last supper with his friends, became the "Liturgy of the Lord's Table" in the Mass.

For the observant Jew, each day was a microcosm of the week and the year. The hours of the day were marked with appropriate ceremony. In Jerusalem, there were sacrifices in the Temple near dawn and sunset. There were certain psalms for different days. These are the roots of the Christian monastic "offices" or "hours" of Lauds (morning prayer) and Vespers (evening prayer). There were also services of psalms and prayers at mid-morning, midday, and mid-afternoon. These were carried into the monks' "Little Hours" of Terce (third hour of the day—9 A.M.), Sext (sixth hour), and None (ninth hour). For both practicing Jew and Christian monk, the cycle of the day was accented with prayerful attempts to remember the presence of God in the community.

There are various ways to start my day. I can refuse to admit that sleep is over. At some point, my laziness turns to panic and a hectic attempt to catch up with the clock. There is little spiritual advantage in this approach. It is no better when I have a tightly organized approach with all my problems and chores in mind. Before I have been up an hour, I can already cross several items off my mental "things-to-do" list. Even morning prayer becomes a task to be performed—so much meditation, so many psalms and prayers. I can go on this way for a while but, in the long run, it is unsatisfying.

When I have nothing to do but become aware of the new day, then I can be open to spiritual nourishment. I live in the country and can walk among trees as the dawn light comes through the branches and wakes up the world around me. When the leaf changes color or the bird sings, I feel my soul being refreshed. But a person does not have to have beautiful trees and pure air. I have watched the dawn light coming through the haze of a polluted sky in an Eastern European city hard hit by an unsuccessful revolution. Never did I feel a greater sense of hope and renewal.

In the early morning, I like a time of quiet meditation in a sacred place. For me, this is usually a little chapel, but it has also been under a tree, in a train, or in the bathroom with the noisy sound of children beyond the door.

It feels good to start the day with a time of reflection. There is not as much resistance to morning meditation and prayer as there is to taking a spiritual break at midday. Once we are in our work mode, we are programmed to grind on until we are exhausted. In rural Europe, the Angelus bells were rung at midday. It was a time for people in the fields to stop and realize that whatever they were doing, it was not the whole picture. Today it is also important to remember there is more to life than our work.

When I am at home, I participate in a communion service at noon. On those times when I am away, I try to remember to make some quiet time. I am impressed by the creativity of people who work in 9 to 5 positions and find a way at noon to take a short spiritual break. One thing I have learned from some of them is the advantage of a slow walk. I try to see things I earlier passed by in my hurry to get to whatever task I was performing. There are flowers in the cracks of the sidewalks, and birds do fly in the sky above the tall buildings. One of my favorite spots in San Francisco is a park in front of an old church. It is surrounded by trendy restaurants where some of the city's movers and shakers come to maximize the advantages of their business lunch. When I am in one of these eateries, there is a sense of high energy. The relentless drive of my fellow diners is often jarring to me. I feel more at home across the street in the park. When the Angelus bell rings, the parochial school students go into the church. The bell also seems to be a signal for old men and women from Chinatown to practice Tai Chi and other forms of graceful spiritual movement. College students munch on bagels, which they share with the birds. All manner of people, some with care etched in their faces, take their places on the benches with the same solemnity as if they were sitting down in a church pew. Actually I feel that way myself. I look around at this open-air congregation and I feel God's presence among us. This too is a holy communion.

As the day moves on, I look forward to Vespers. It is a wonderful time in a small spiritual community like ours. The day's work is over. Light is fading. The word "Vespers" comes from the Latin for "evening star." It is an ancient service probably rooted in Jewish tradition. After a day of crossing tasks off a list, it is sweet to regain a broader perspective by singing together the psalms and listening to the readings and prayers.

The Anglican community very appropriately refers to this prayer as "Evensong," but this soft evening time of song is not always available to me when I am caring for the children. As the kids get out of school, my "second day" begins, as it does for millions of other parents. All the victories and trials of their day must be absorbed, as well as handling the logistical tangles resulting from the notes and announcements that the teachers send home. After a snack comes a playtime when they can unwind. Doctor appointments, extracurricular activities, and trips to replace the broken thermos bottle are fitted in somewhere. There is dinner to prepare, followed by help with homework, getting ready for bed, stories to read, deep confidences to share, stars to look at, prayers to say. A parent of school-aged children is really unlikely to find an hour for Vespers, but fifteen minutes is often possible.

What works best for me is to take a few minutes before the dinner is prepared. The kids know that this short time is important for me. They go in their rooms or to the yard and play or do homework. I sit in the now calm living room, choose a psalm at random, read it, and spend a few moments in quiet reflection. It is an arbitrary ritual. I think anything would do. The point at these hectic times is for me to remember I have a spiritual rhythm to my life. In Benedict's rule for monks, he acknowledges that sometimes a person must miss a chapel service—in which case "the decided upon hours should not pass them by." It is not so much what we do but that we take a moment to break the chain of activities and remind ourselves there is more to our lives.

A friend of mine begins her short spiritual break with the simple question, "In the last days of my life, what will I recall from this day?" It is a good question.

Compline, or Night Prayer, originated with early monastic communities as a service to end the day. In winter, the monks would gather in the one heated room to warm up for the night. They would then go to the chapel for Compline and a final blessing by the abbot. This was the beginning of the "Great Silence," which would bring total quiet to the night. Most people today have several endings to the day. The younger children go to bed at one time, we stop answering the phone at another, the TV is turned off, or the book we are reading is shut even later. There never is a "great" silence to the night, simply little ones. Still, something of the Compline service can be savored.

After dinner, in our family, we sometimes gather for a hymn, a short Bible reading or poem, a time of quiet, a prayer, and a blessing. We often substitute a silent walk outside to view the moon, marvel at the stars, or listen to the sounds of the night.

I always have a lot of thoughts as the day ends. Many years ago I tried to collect some of them in the only prayer I have ever composed:

> O Gentle One, you are our trust, the stillness in whom there is no change. Call us home from wherever we may have wandered. Help us to discard the memories of our busyness, that in simplicity we may rediscover the wonder of your way. Heal our hurts and protect our joys. Guide us to the peace of your presence and help us to find rest in the warmth of your love. Amen.

We can wear ourselves out responding to the changes we face in everyday life. There must be periodic points when we quit spinning and refresh ourselves. People have known this for centuries. Like most people today, I have to be frequently reminded.

✳ Blessing Our Children ✳

A child's primary spiritual center is the home. A number of years ago I wrote an article for *Parents Magazine* titled "Bless Your Kid!," which advocated a return to the old practice of family blessings. It had a strong positive reaction from the readers. In the article, I used examples from some of the families I have known and respected over the years.

Rosa, a single parent, was not an especially religious person. She stopped attending church regularly when she entered college. After a divorce, she worked hard to maintain the sense of family. In Rosa's own childhood, the Hispanic tradition of parental blessing had helped her to see her own mother as a bridge between the family and the larger community. None of Rosa's four children left for school without a blessing. Being uncomfortable with too much "God talk," Rosa simply put her hands on each child's head and said: "May you grow today in peace and wisdom." It became a powerful memory for her kids.

The custom of parents blessing their children can be found in most cultures. The practice has deep roots in the Judeo-Christian heritage. It was an important aspect of inheritance, as we learned when Jacob deceived his blind father Isaac into giving him a blessing intended for his brother Esau (Genesis 27). We still retain references in our language to asking for a parent's blessing on a marriage or other major ventures in life. A parent's blessing is simply a spiritual hug. There are countless moments in parenting when we reach out to a child. None are as poignant as when the daughter or son we love is seriously ill.

Sara was a bright and active ten-year-old. She was riding her bicycle home from school, wearing her helmet, when she was struck by a speeding car. For several days, Sara's father and mother were at her hospital bed as she drifted in and out of consciousness. The doctors were unsure of the future. Dan, Sara's father, was an active person who had trouble accepting that there was nothing he or anyone else could do. Late one night the nurse checked the tubes feeding Sara, pulled back the curtain dividing the quiet room, and left. After a few minutes, Sara slowly opened her eyes. Dan knew the look of confusion, but before either he or his wife could say a word of reassurance, Sara's eyes closed. Without thinking, Dan stood up and went to the bed. He placed his big hands gently but solidly on Sara's bandaged head. He did not say anything. In a moment, he felt his wife's presence on the other side of the bed. Her graceful hands now joined his in the silence. Whatever strength they had was being offered to their daughter. In the weeks that followed, Sara improved. Months later, when asked about her memories of those bad times, Sara once said that she remembered the time when "Mom and Dad gave me everything they had."

Like Sara's parents, we all have times when we want to give something inside us to a child. Sometimes we wonder if it is wanted—probably it is. Rusty was the kind of teenager who usually got his way. He had argued and whined until his parents agreed to let him take a raft trip down a wild river. Rusty knew this trip was a bigger physical challenge than he had ever faced before. When the morning for his departure arrived, he hesitated at the door before joining a waiting carload of friends. "Hey, Mom," he called to his worried mother, "wish me luck." Like all the young people in history before him, Rusty was asking for a blessing before beginning an important adventure. He was not surprised when his mother took his face in her hands. There was not even the customary annoyed look as she prayed out loud. In fact, at some deep level

Rusty knew that she really meant it when she said: "May God bless you, protect you, and be with you." It was a simple ritual, which, at that moment, came naturally to both mother and son.

One of the important spiritual skills parents can teach children is the ability to find something special in an ordinary moment. The most common remnant of an ancient blessing is the phrase, "Good night." This formula has its roots in the prayers for the protection of all who were to share a night together under the same roof. In most homes, the moment before sleep is the most natural for a parent's blessing.

Anna was still a baby when her mother began to hold her as an ending to the day. When Anna was a toddler, her father joined in the ritual. It was a simple matter. After Anna was in bed, her parents sat on either side and silently held her hands. The practice continued into school age. Basically there was no difference between this nightly blessing and a good-night kiss except for a little more time in which the family could silently share their love. As she grew older, Anna continued to sense that each evening her parents were drawing her into that mysterious adult world that would one day be hers. In the later grades, there was too much competition at bedtime and the time together was often missed. In high school it was finally abandoned altogether.

When Anna was in college, she began to question the religious values of her childhood. She developed a serious interest in Zen Buddhism. This was painful to her parents who were deeply involved in their own spiritual tradition and had little understanding of Eastern religions. Anna wanted their approval for her quest but understood their sorrow. After graduation, she decided to become a full-time Zen student in a West Coast center. This was the first major experience of Anna's life in which her parents could not find some way to share. On the day of her flight to California, the gap between the three of them seemed immense. Just before they went to the airport, her mother and father sat down beside Anna on the couch. They felt awkward. Without thinking, Anna offered her hand to her mother. In a few moments, her father took her other hand. The experience of all those evening blessings during childhood let their mutual love and respect transcend the gulf between them. Without a word, Anna received the blessing she desired and her parents knew that a part of them was going with her into this strange new world.

10

Sacred Seasons

Frosty spider webs, apple blossoms, the song of a meadowlark, the sound of water, wind in the trees, the sight of the morning star are all wonders that lead me to an awareness of the sacred and help me understand my place in the changing rhythms of history.

When I live close to the land, like our ancient ancestors, the seasons of the year solicit a spiritual response. If I am involved in more abstract activities, I often have to be prompted to live in harmony with nature's cycles. Reminders come from the arts as well as from spiritual traditions. Greek drama grew out of seasonal agricultural liturgies. In Japanese haiku poetry, the poet located himself in the poem by way of the season. The yearly liturgical cycle, in tandem with the arts, is also a practical support for my spiritual growth.

The church year for Christians evolved from Jewish traditions that were based upon annual rural realities. Great festivals were associated with specific events: Passover with the new flocks, Pentecost with the wheat harvest, Tabernacles with the new wine. And yet there were always levels of meaning beyond agriculture. Passover, for example, commemorates the exodus from slavery and the entrance into the promised land. Christians see the death and resurrection of Jesus as a similar liberation.

After Christianity became the established religion in Rome, certain former pagan feasts, especially those associated with the winter solstice, were absorbed into the Christian year. Thus, for example, the birthday of Jesus was substituted for the birthday of Solis Invicti—the Unconquerable Sun. Seasonal observances, both Christian and non-Christian, can be uniquely enriching.

Winter

For many of us, the spiritual year begins in winter. Everything seems dead. Nature is working in secret. The Hopi people in Arizona go down into sacred places dug into the earth and pray over the seeds they will later plant, in recognition of the fact that life begins in the womb of the earth. On the same winter nights, I walk on top of the land where leafless trees are silhouetted against the full moon. Somewhere in those bare limbs is life. New buds will swell when the time is right. Some nights I can understand that my spiritual life has the same latent vitality. One of my favorite Advent hymns is "People Look East, The Time Is Near." The old French melody has a more modern text which proclaims in one verse: "Furrows be glad. Though the earth is bare, one more seed is planted there . . . ."[17]

"Advent" (in Latin *adventus*) means "coming." It begins near the first of December and is a time of joyful expectation celebrating both the event of Jesus' first coming and the building of God's kingdom on earth in our own age. Advent reflects the interrelation between the natural world and the spiritual.

The major symbol of Advent is light. It is a powerful time for me when our little spiritual community gathers in the darkened chapel and we light the first candle on the Advent wreath. Like everyone else, I have been wounded in the process of living. These pains often come up to the surface in the darkness of a late December afternoon. When the first candle on the wreath is lit, the light helps push back the darkness and the pain. The challenge of Advent is to learn how to bring more light and joy to the world.

The fourth-century Bishop Nicholas of Myra, in Asia Minor, has long been associated with Christmas. Five hundred years after his death, charming stories about him were collected, including an account of his throwing three bags of gold through the window of a man who had no money to provide wedding dowries for his three daughters. The feast day of St. Nicholas is December 6. The eve of that day is a significant event in The Netherlands and many other places in Europe. In my home, we celebrate the eve of St. Nicholas on a convenient date near December 5. Mostly it is a time to let the children's excitement be channeled by a few toys and treats and a visit from the mysterious old bishop. He has a list of the children's misdeeds, which is always outnumbered by the list of their good deeds. Each Saturday lunch after St. Nicholas Day is a time for a discussion on what we can do together to make a better world. In a modest way, our actions go along with an old German children's rhyme:

> Who is running through the town?
> Who is knocking on the judge's door?
> That is Bishop Nicholas,
>> fighting for justice.
> He did not let the great ones of his time
>> rest and sleep in peace.
> Nicholas, run! Nicholas, run!
> Wake up the self-satisfied, the unjust
>> the lazy people.
> Wake up all of us!

Sometimes I have to be shaken out of my cynicism and disgust at the commercialism of Christmas. It has gone back to being a pagan carnival. When Charles Dickens wrote *A Christmas Carol* in 1843, he mixed about 85 percent fear and misery with 15 percent plum pudding. Today the goal is zero pain, 100 percent plum pudding. I increasingly find the result emotionally indigestible. Christmas is a potential healing time. A carnival is a way of denying you have anything to heal. For myself, I frequently need solace at this time of year. I take no comfort from the plastic reindeer, the "HO-HO-HO" chants, and the gatherings of people straining to act out their festive roles.

Winter is not always a wonderland. It is also a hard time for beings living on the margin of life. This includes a broad spectrum of folks: both people and animals without homes, the old and the sick whose immune systems are weakened, little creatures who can find no food in the cold ground, those who are lonely and sad and forgotten. These beings must be included for there to be an authentic community celebration. I must be aware of them as well as the aspects of my own being that are alien, sick, hungry, bittersweet.

Healing can come to me after being alone with a fir tree in the dawn light, gazing at the stars, watching a fire. Perhaps the essence of Advent for me is making room for the sacred. John of the Cross (1542-1591) has a sweet little poem which says, in part:

> The virgin, pregnant with the Divine Word,
> Will come strolling down your road,
> If you make room for her
> In your abode.

There is a special strength I get from singing the old hymns and reading poems written in winter. The most ancient are some from the eighth century, sung at the evening services during the week before Christmas. These are called the "O Antiphons" because the original Latin texts all began with "O." On successive days we sing for Wisdom to lead us, for God who was the light of Israel, for the Flower of Jesse's lineage to come quickly, for the Key of David to lead us out from the prison of fear, for the Morning Star of justice, for the King of All Nations, for Emmanuel—God with us. That takes us to the day before Christmas, which is best for me as a quiet day. I like to walk and to become more aware of the story of nature at this time of solstice. I take a child with me in the, often fruitless, attempt to lead her to a stillpoint in the cyclone of holiday excitement.

In the evening, Christmas Eve, the constellation Orion is directly overhead. I like to reflect on a passage from the Book of Wisdom (18:14):

> When peaceful silence lay over all,
> and night had run the half of her swift course,
> down from the heavens, from the royal throne,
> leapt your all-powerful Word.

Our simple chapel service starts with a single violin playing "Silent Night, Holy Night." In our own vulnerability, the women, men, and children have gathered to remember the vulnerable child on whom our people's hopes rested. John Donne wrote in a sonnet that Jesus was in Mary's womb until he became "Weake enough, now into our world to come."

This great event of the divine and the human merging took place in a barn. The story directs us not to the halls of the powerful but to common, and even trivial aspects of ordinary life. Yet it is a time of awe and wonder—as is the birth of any child.

Coming out of the chapel into the cold night and walking under the stars, I sense we have experienced the God-child being born in each of us.

For most of the commercial world the holiday ends at sundown on December 25. It should be just beginning. The Twelve Days of Christmas, from Christmas Day to Epiphany, were the prolongation of the Holy Night in days gone by. It is a good tradition. There needs to be some time free of the gift-giving and partying to experience the simple sense of birth and new life in the midst of a barren world. Today a growing number of offices may be recognizing this need by closing down between Christmas and New Year's. In my home we gather around the fireplace each evening and, after belting out yet another rendition of "The Twelve Days of Christmas," listen to stories told or read by different people that reflect varied aspects of the festival. Each year I have a renewed understanding of what a rich mosaic Christmas can be.

The season effectively ends with Epiphany, which is celebrated on January 6 or the nearest Sunday. "Epiphany" means "the manifestation." In the Eastern church, Epiphany celebrated everything connected to God's breaking into humanity through the person of Jesus. Later in the Western church, when the birth of Jesus was celebrated on December 25, Epiphany was associated with the visit of the wise men—the magi. To me, it is an echo of Christmas and renews the promise that there is new life in our world. There is a little admonition here to those of us who try to think everything out. The shepherds, with their simple hearts, reached the child before the learned magi.

Spring

The English word "Lent" comes from a term meaning "springtime" or, more precisely, "the lengthening of the days."

Many medieval monks would fast, pray, and do continual acts of penance from Epiphany to Easter. Fasting can be a good and purifying practice, as in the Islamic sacred month of Ramadan, but I have sometimes wondered if fasting was a solution to the shortage of food in medieval monasteries at that time of year. In any event, during the Middle Ages, the attitude of a penitential marathon spilled over into the celebration of Lent. This is in contrast to the early years of the Christian community when the time before Easter was the period for new converts to prepare for baptism and a new life of the spirit. The theme was renewal not penance, and it related to the freshness of spring. Preparing for Easter in this fashion is an annual nourishment I value.

In my home there is the custom of eating up "Old Man Winter." A big gingerbread cookie is covered with white frosting. On some sunny day toward the beginning of Lent, the children slowly eat up the Old Man and proclaim the end of winter with a quote from the Song of Songs (2:11-13):

> For see, winter is past,
> the rains are over and gone.
> The flowers appear on the earth.
> The season of glad songs has come,
> the cooing of the turtle dove
> is heard in our land.

The biblical idea of putting off the "the old person" and putting on "the new person" is not so far away from this children's ritual of renewal. And who is to say that biblical heroes did not occasionally enjoy a cookie?

The "new person" should be less self-centered than the old one. This can be a central theme for Lenten renewal. Acts of fasting and piety are no doubt good for individual spiritual growth but are they very interesting to God? Not according to Isaiah (58:5-9), who has God saying to us:

> Fasting like yours today
> will never make your voice heard on high . . .
> Is not this the sort of fast that pleases me . . .
> to break unjust fetters
> to undo the thongs of the yoke,
> to let the oppressed go free, . . .
> to share your bread with the hungry
> to shelter the homeless poor,
> to clothe the person you see to be naked
> and not turn from your own kin?

Participating in the new life of spring and giving a hand where it is needed is a good way to prepare for the great events commemorated and recreated in the bittersweet themes of Holy Week.

Even with all the blossoms on the trees and new flowers breaking through the earth, death is always with us. The blossom must fall before the fruit can come. There can be no Easter without the cross. In the back of my mind during Lent, there is always an awareness of the death of Jesus and the destruction of the innocent in our own day, which can never be completely masked by the beauty of the spring countryside.

Holy Week is an icon for facts in life I would prefer to ignore. One of those realities is the continual destruction of beauty by those who worship power and are threatened by anything they cannot control.

The week begins with Palm Sunday, which is now officially known as "Passion Sunday" because one of the gospel accounts of Jesus' suffering and death are read out in churches at that time. We sing "Hosanna," which is Hebrew for "May God save." It is how people are said to have acclaimed Jesus when he entered Jerusalem. They waved palm and olive branches. This is the same crowd who turned on Jesus later in the week when he did not meet their expectations. I think that is still going on. It is "my friend and brother Jesus" until I become convinced that Jesus is not teaching what I want to hear or is failing to do what I want done. Then I turn away.

Palms were associated with blessings. In some services, each person goes around the church holding a palm over other's heads and blessing them. Sometimes the palms are exchanged as a further way of sharing the blessings. Once Tina, my almost three-year-old adopted daughter, was very sick from AIDS during the Palm Sunday service. She was carried around during the service, but she had no strength and had collapsed on her mother's shoulder. They were standing next to me as the palms were exchanged. I had my back to them until I felt a little hand on my arm. I turned and looked into Tina's blue eyes. Her head was up and she was holding out a palm to exchange with mine. She took the moment very seriously and so have I ever since that day. Tina died a few days later. We saved and framed the palm she gave me. It comes out in the chapel every Palm Sunday.

The first few days of Holy Week can be a quiet time for reflection. Since the society in which most of us exist no longer observes this time, it is hard to retreat completely from the noise and busyness of ordinary life. But just the awareness of the fact that many consider this a holy time makes it easier to turn toward the quiet center of our lives. When I am at home, it is easier to find a gentle rhythm. In the chapel, we sing the poems attributed to Jeremiah lamenting the destruction of Jerusalem. At the dinner table, we bring to mind the long and often tragic story of the people of Israel, Jesus' people, down to the present day. Outside we are putting flower plants in the beds and pots and trying to keep unnecessary busyness to a minimum.

The three major days of Holy Week, the Easter Triduum, begin on Thursday evening. Elaborate rituals are conducted in large churches and cathedrals, but more and more small communities and families are adapting simpler alternatives that capture the essence of the days in a refreshing richness.

The theme for Holy Thursday is love. Jesus gave the commandment to love one another as he loved us. That love was demonstrated at the last supper Jesus had with his friends. We have prolonged that moment by the eucharistic celebrations among the people of God throughout the centuries. The practice was already well established by the time Paul gave his instructions on "The Lord's Supper" around A.D. 50 (1 Corinthians 11:23-26):

> For this is what I received from the Lord, and in turn passed on to you: that on the same night that he was betrayed, the Lord Jesus took some bread, and thanked God for it and broke it, and he said, "This is my body, which is for you; do this as a memorial of me." In the same way he took the cup after supper, and said "This cup is the new covenant in my blood. Whenever you drink it, do this as a memorial of me."

Jesus was celebrating a domestic religious meal with his closest friends. The ritual called for the use of bread and wine. He referred to them as his body and blood. In biblical terms, "blood" did not simply mean what was in the veins and arteries but referred to the vitality of the whole living person—life.

The Holy Thursday service ends abruptly. It is a jarring moment. Where did all the warm fellowship of the meal go? This is much like the life most of us lead. A happy experience, a lovely world, followed by the crashing news of an accident, cancer, heart attack, AIDS, war, the stray bullet of a gang fight, the exploitation of labor and bodies.

I am sometimes afraid to say to myself, "What a wonderful life I have!" So often afterward comes news of the death of a child or an old friend. But this is the very rhythm of Holy Week. As with music, life has movements. The first may be joyful, the second could be sorrowful. That is the way it has to be. I cannot keep playing the first movement over and over. I must move on to the second. But the music does not end there. There is a third movement yet to come.

The night between Holy Thursday and Good Friday commemorates a horrible time for Jesus and his friends. He was arrested, his trial and suffering began, his companions denied him. The happy little world of Jesus of Nazareth was crushed when it came up against the "real world" of the political and religious establishment.

Good Friday is a quiet day of fasting. I can never remember a Good Friday that was rainy or stormy. I am sure there have been, but my sense of the day is a peaceful warm day. Its niceness is what makes the story of oppression then, and now, so real to me. Bad things often happen in lovely settings. If Jesus had looked out a window he would have seen a beautiful day beckoning. But he could not come.

Standing alone, Jesus heard the dread words from the Roman stranger who controlled his life. He was to die. In a few hours, his life would be no more. There would be no more walks on the green hills, no more listening to the sound of the waves, no more smiles of friends, no more quiet moments by the fire. Only pain and death remained. Why?

Jesus ignored the establishment when he announced the coming of the Kingdom. He invited the poor and the outcasts to be as happy as the privileged classes. This was wonderful for the little people. But it made the great ones uncomfortable. And there was more. Jesus showed that he knew God. He announced that the Father was no mysterious hidden king; he was a warm and caring "Abba"—a Dad who freely acknowledges that he belongs to us and we to him. This was heard as blasphemy, an unforgivable indignity to God. Only the official leaders were authorized to announce God's will and law.

Jesus was also a threat to Rome. He was not a big threat, but a threat nonetheless. This odd Jew was a nuisance to the law and order of society. Wherever he went while in Jerusalem, there was a disturbance. He was an irritant that could be removed.

For disturbances to the comfortableness of society, Jesus would die and be shown up for what he was—a nothing. He would die the humiliating death reserved for the lowest of creatures. Through the centuries, countless men and women have been removed from the sunlight in one way or another because they dared to be themselves and ignored the rules of the game. Yet their silent suffering has often contributed greatly to the unfolding of life in future ages.

I would always like to skip over what happened to Jesus at the hands of the Roman soldiers. Wars in the classical world were only won with fearsome brutality. Warriors did not like gentle folk who said things like "Blessed are the peacemakers for they shall be called the children of God." The soldiers stripped Jesus naked and tied him to a post. The blows came one after another. Romans killed their condemned enemies by whipping them almost to death and then hanging their near dead bodies on a cross as an example to all the critics of Rome. Death was slow and painful. Always efficient, it was considered practical by the Romans for the prisoner to carry the crossbeam of his cross. This was tied to the back of the condemned man. There were many crucifixions in those days, and the vertical timbers were simply left in place.

When they cut Jesus down from the whipping post, there was little life left in him. Still, he was made to enter the jeering crowd, stumbling along with the heavy timber. It is doubtful that he noticed the faces of the crowd. If he had any earthly thought, it was probably for the pain he was suffering. There actually would not have been many in the crowd with hatred in their eyes. Most would be happy and laughing. Everyone was in a holiday spirit. The suffering of Jesus was just one of the sideshows for the country people coming into the big city of Jerusalem at this festive time of Passover. In fact, for some it must have been sport to see the soldiers prodding the prisoner along. After all, everyone knew that people condemned to death were bad people and fair game.

Most of the crowd would have passed on after a few minutes to see the other marvels of the city. I cannot blame them. Around me are often people in pain, people whose world has collapsed. I pass them by with hardly a glance. If anything, they are an inconvenience, a disturbance.

Jesus was weakening. If the soldiers were ever to get him up to the place of execution, they would have to get someone else to carry that heavy timber. He simply could not make it. They drafted Simon of Cyrene out of the crowd. I have a fantasy the soldiers may have been outwitted. It is at least possible the man they grabbed may have put himself where he could have been chosen. His sons, we are told, were known to the early Christians. His wife may later have befriended Paul. Perhaps Simon had even taunted the soldiers about how slowly everything was going, until in frustration one of them said, "All right, then, you carry it."

In my imagination, I have constructed a picture of Simon. I think he was a simple man. Before this fateful day he may have listened, but only half understood, the discussions between his sons and their intellectual friends as they related the significance of Jesus in history. Perhaps Simon was not even sure he was a follower of Jesus. Yet he had the courage to be there when others fled. He could well understand the needs of a man in deep trouble. He knew what to do and he did it. Carrying the cross was a task to perform, and Simon was a man used to hard work.

It was probable that Jesus did not even know what was happening at this point, but once the impossible weight of the timber was lifted from him he could focus his remaining energy on what was to come. He could muster the dignity he needed to convert this atrocity into one of the great spiritual acts of the ages.

Jesus was stripped naked again. Rough hands held his arms as the long spikes were driven through his wrists on to the crossbeam. He was hauled up, his flesh torn apart and his brain exploding with pain. His ankles were nailed down. His young body was now completely violated. All that remained was to wait for him to die, from the vicious whipping, exhaustion, and thirst.

On the cross of shame, Jesus had nothing. Everything was taken away. He was powerless, unable to remove even one of the hordes of insects that crawled over the open wounds of his body or to hide anything from the eyes of those who passed by. He hung between heaven and earth. In desperation, he raised his voice to God using the first words of a psalm, "My God, my God, why have you deserted me?" Around the cross, a deep stillness had descended and touched the hearts of those few who watched. Now, at last, some people were beginning to awaken.

What a strange image for the world—a crucified sage. Yet out of this hour came a new hope for the human race. The cross, the symbol of shame, would become a sign of glory. These few friends watching this event would grow to a great fellowship that has lasted through the centuries. No one will ever truly know how that happened.

When death comes to someone we love, nature usually numbs our senses until we can better handle the loss. Holy Saturday is that kind of experience. I have a sense of relief that the intensity of Good Friday is over. I welcome an emotional buffer in order to absorb the next phase of this remarkable week. In my community, we spend Saturday preparing for the celebration of Easter. One of the most important little rituals for me is planting bright colored flowers around the place. It is especially pleasing when I am working with the children and we can talk about the meaning of Easter—the first one and this one.

The English word "Easter" is derived from an Old English variation of "Eostra," a goddess of spring. Her name connotes the dawn, which comes in the east. The basic idea of all east-words is "the shining." Easter, the dawning of the spring, is the shining season following the dull season of winter. Most European languages use a word, like the Greek *Pascha*, which can be traced back to the Jewish Passover (in Hebrew *pesach*), a celebration of the redemption from slavery combined with a Canaanite agricultural festival. This was the background for Jesus' last supper with his friends. By the second century, the Christian church was referring to Jesus as the lamb sacrificed in order to obtain deliverance from the slavery of sin and the finality of death.

In paintings and stained-glass windows, we see Jesus, bathed in light, floating up from the tomb. But the gospels describe only an empty tomb, not his body rising. What does it mean? That will always be a mystery. There was a strong understanding among Jesus' followers that death was not the final word. Watching Jesus die on the cross had produced despair among his friends. Yet in some way Jesus was not destroyed by death.

The authorities did not accept that Jesus had risen from the dead, but they had to accept that his influence was stronger after his crucifixion than before. Jesus' message was spread through his followers, and it would be impossible to say he was not, in some way, in their midst.

Many Christians, all over the world, celebrate the Easter Vigil at some time between sunset on Saturday and dawn on Sunday. Our community begins about 4:30 A.M. We have adapted many ancient ceremonies. In the darkness of the night a new fire leaps into the sky. The large Easter candle is lit and from it each person's candle until there is light again among us. We read the old stories of liberation from the Old Testament and the gospels. Water collected from a pristine spring recalls our baptism, the bread and wine make us aware of the presence of God among us. We greet the dawn, and each other, overflowing with alleluias. Solemnness gives way to simple joy. The meaning of this great story is that we can move out of the shadows and play in the light. The children in their bright clothes hunt for eggs. They bring their baskets to a great festive breakfast. The table is covered with flowers and pretty things. Someplace along the line, our family started collecting Russian dolls that open to reveal smaller and smaller dolls within. These come out at breakfast. They are a good symbol of Easter. Our spiritual life keeps going down and down to the very core of our being, and of God's.

The Easter joy of being alive and somehow partners with God goes on for seven weeks. The season ends with the feast of Pentecost where we celebrate the gift of the Holy Spirit, the comforter who is always with us. This facet of the divine mystery is what the Old Testament calls "Wisdom." And Wisdom is always a "she." Her symbol has come to be the dove and her sound is the wind. She is the breath of life. We hear it all around us: in the trees, across the fields, in the words we speak.

With the memory of the sweet wind and the flowers of spring, we walk into the summer.

Summer and Autumn

After Pentecost, in the language of the liturgical cycle, we enter into "Ordinary Time." It is a wonderful phrase. Ordinary time is the real world for most of us. The time of "nothing special." A Zen master described the same concept as:

> Before enlightenment:
> > gathering wood and carrying water.
>
> After enlightenment:
> > gathering wood and carrying water.

In the long hot days of summer, the fruit ripens on the trees. There is work to be done. The summer solstice is in late June. After that, each day gets a little shorter. Soon the harvest time approaches and we have the beautiful moons of late summer. At the time of the Lammas (August) moon, bread was once made from newly harvested grains. There are many grains but only one loaf. It is a symbol of the many peoples who make one people of God.

The first chill in the evening air calls us to our homes, our centers, as the Japanese haiku poet Issa (1763-1827) wrote:

> In the autumn wind,
> The compass points
> Of its own accord
> To my village home.[18]

Harvest time comes and with it giving thanks to the providence that provides the water, and the sunshine, and the plants we need.

School begins and the rhythm of life changes. Nature's wheel is turning again. Even in large cities, the trees turn color and the leaves fall and play with us in the streets. At my home, we have a Festival of Leaves. The children gather them and bring them to the chapel one Sunday.

There are many ancient saint's days at this time of year. Among them are, Michaelmas (September 29), St. Francis (October 4), All Saints (November 1), and All Souls (November 2). They each present a facet of the gospel in concrete terms. Martinmas is on November 11. The days are getting colder and the needs of those in want are more severe. Martin of Tours (316/17-397) is remembered for sharing his cloak with a shivering beggar who later turned out to be Jesus. There is a venerable Gaelic rune of hospitality associated with St. Martin's day:

> I saw a stranger yesterday.
> I put food in the eating place—
> drink in the drinking place—
> and in the blessed name of God,
> he blessed myself and my house,
> my cattle and my dear ones.
> And the lark said in her song:
> "often, often, often goes Christ
> in the stranger's guise."

The days are short. The light is dimming, but we know it will return. Until then, the lack of light will let us see and feel and, according to some of the earth's first peoples, hear the stars.

Now the cycle begins all over again. And each of us journeys on in company with every woman, man, and child on this planet. Together we quest for the sacred.

✳ Works of Compassion ✳

For various reasons, we in the privileged first world are losing our ability to look beyond our own individual desires in order to seek the common good. As a result, our personal spiritual needs will be unfulfilled because none of us can satisfy those needs while focusing only on our individual selves. Compassion is not an altruistic luxury but a fundamental necessity for each of us if we are to grow spiritually.

The word "compassion" comes from a Latin root that means "to suffer with another." It is a recognition of a shared human condition. Compassion is not pity. I can pity and help another. I give my help with gratitude that the other person's plight is not mine. In the first years of the AIDS pandemic, the suffering of homosexuals and drug users with AIDS was so horrible that American Christian congregations were asked to take pity on them. They were, by and large, willing to do that, but it was clearly an "us"/"them" situation. A conference of Catholic educators was stunned when a respected speaker announced, in those early days, "The Church has AIDS." His point was this was not a time for pity. There were no "them" and "us."

There was only "we"—and "we" had AIDS.

When I was young, we had to memorize many things as we made our way through the stepping stones of promised salvation in the Catholic Church. One task was to recite the *Works of Mercy*, which were divided into *corporal* and *spiritual*. After reciting them to the catechism teacher, we would receive a star on the proper line of our progress chart. Then we probably put them out of mind. That was unfortunate because they are good spiritual guidelines if we really live by them.

The *Corporal Works of Mercy* have strong scriptural roots. They start with an exasperated God in Isaiah (58:6-11) who, as I mentioned in the previous chapter, lets it be known he has no interest whatsoever in people covering themselves with sackcloth and ashes, moping about, and fasting. Forget all that stuff. What pleases God is for people:

> to break unjust fetters
> and undo the thongs of the yoke,
> to let the oppressed go free,
> and break every yoke,
> to share your bread with the hungry,
> and shelter the homeless poor,

to clothe the person you see to be naked
and not turn from your own kin . . .
If you do away with the yoke,
the clenched fist, the wicked word,
if you give your bread to the hungry,
and relief to the oppressed,
your light will rise in the darkness,
and your shadows become like noon.
Yahweh will always guide you,
giving you relief in desert places.

This is not just a process for building up credits in some heavenly bank account. We are being urged to recognize that this is the way we find God in our lives. Jesus restates this position clearly when he speaks (Matthew 25:24-40) of his encountering the human race at the end of time:

I was hungry and you gave me food; I was
thirsty and you gave me drink; I was a stranger
and you made me welcome; naked and you
clothed me, sick and you visited me, in prison
and you came to see me.

This confused the people, who could not remember having helped him. Jesu s then said that "in so far as you did this to one of the least of these members of my family, you did it to me." If we want to encounter the divine element in our lives, we must develop a compassionate response to our brothers and sisters, which is, in turn, a way of recognizing that we are dependent on each other. From earliest times, followers of Jesus were urged:

To feed the hungry
To give drink to the thirsty
To clothe the naked
To visit the imprisoned
To give shelter to the homeless
To visit the sick
To bury the dead.

The more a person practices and reflects on these *Corporal Works of Mercy*, the more profound they become. I have not often encountered naked people in the streets, but I have often found persons who have been stripped of their dignity or ability to cope with life. It is rare now that I visit a jail, but frequently I do find people imprisoned by old age, sickness, poverty, or marginalized by an uncaring society.

The *Spiritual Works of Mercy* are also pulled out of scripture and address the special spiritual and emotional needs of us all:

To admonish the wayward.

If your brother does something wrong go
and have it out with him alone (Matthew 18:15).

To instruct the uninformed.

To support the doubtful.

Happy are those who have not seen me and
yet have faith (John 20:29).

To be present to the sorrowful.

To bear wrongs patiently.

Think of a farmer: how patiently he waits for the
precious fruit of the ground until he has had the
autumn rains and the spring rains! You too have to
be patient (James 5:7).

To forgive injuries.

If you forgive others their failings, your heavenly
Father will forgive you yours (Matthew 6:15).

To pray for the living and the dead.

It must be recognized that some of these guidelines in the *Spiritual Works of Mercy* were used through the centuries to prolong oppression in an unhealthy alliance between the church and the power establishment. Serfs and laborers were told to be patient. Their reward would be in heaven. This is obviously not what Jesus had in mind.

As with the *Corporal Works of Mercy,* there are layers of meaning as we attempt to apply these spiritual guidelines in our daily lives. For example, support of "the doubtful" is welcome on those many occasions when we doubt our worth, our relationships, our path. Several of these *Spiritual Works of Mercy* require us to have the courage to become involved when it would be easier to walk away. That involvement can take many forms: advice, support, good example, a gentle presence.

In Matthew's account of the Sermon on the Mount, Jesus is reported to have admonished us to "be perfect just as your heavenly Father is perfect" (Matthew 5:48). Is that possible? Luke's rendition of the same event brings us back to daily life. We are told to "Be compassionate as your Father is compassionate" (Luke 6:36).

A compassionate recognition of God in other people is central to understanding and following Jesus. In chapter 6, I described Jesus as a "bod-hisattva," one of the divine people in the Buddhist tradition who has a compassionate interest in helping all of us. In chapter 7, I have also cited Dietrich Bonhoeffer, who called Jesus "a man for others." We cannot be only for others. It is true we need a sense of self and a personal awareness of the sacred. But in order to grow spiritually, we must recognize that what we have in common with each other is more important than that which separates us.

Sacred Moments

An increased sense of wholeness comes whenever we try to touch some sacred space in our lives, our society, or our history. These efforts are not always labeled as "prayer," but that is what they are. "Prayer," for me, is any attempt to experience the divine element in our lives, any awareness of the presence of God, any longing to find peace in the depths of our being.

Teresa of Avila (1515-1582) compared praying to watering a garden. Sometimes you have to carry buckets from a well and this can be burdensome. At other times, it is possible to design and use an irrigation system. Sometimes it simply rains and we don't have to do anything.

Prayer can often be spontaneous and rooted in our past. I like the story about a horseshoe Isaac Newton (1642-1727) kept over his front door. When anyone asked if he really believed in that good-luck superstition, he would respond, "No, I don't—but I'm told it works anyway."

In my life there have been times of primal expression that have overridden my ordinary preferences in prayer. One such experience occurred at my mother's death. She was in her eighties and had been ill for some time. She died at home during the night of Christmas Eve, as had my father some years before. On Christmas Day, some of us went to the nearby ocean. We sat down for an hour and thought of her life. There were many little prayers and silent meditations. On the drive home, I felt something building up inside me. My last parent was gone. There was nothing between me and history, the future, the cosmos. I felt a need to make a contact with the power of life itself. I went up on a hill behind the house to a place where my mother loved to sit. It was as if her quieted spirit was laying there. I stood over that spirit facing the valley and the far hills. Then a roar began in me and erupted out of my mouth. I could not believe this was happening. A tiny part of my brain was saying, "This is bizarre!" Yet the roars kept coming out and echoed against the hills. I was mourning in some ancient way, and it was the right thing to do. There was no doubt that my mother was with God, and for those few moments, so was I. Then there was a deep and healing silence.

Prayer is very natural during times of sorrow and pain, but it may return us to the simpler spirituality of childhood.

When I sat helpless beside a child whose life was ebbing away, all I could focus on was the first prayer I had learned, the "Our Father." I did not think about the words. The prayer became a mantra I repeated to help me stay in that space I can only describe as heaven opening up. At such fundamental times, there is seldom any doubt about the presence of God.

To bring our actions into harmony with implanted divine grace, it is helpful to begin young. But early experiences in prayer can be negative. A few years ago, I asked a number of young adults about early memories of prayer. Many remembered being uncomfortable when their hands were shoved together or moved by an adult in the sign of the cross. Almost all recalled boredom with the word prayers used in rituals. However, many lovingly recounted simple "prayerful times" when being held up to see the stars, or sitting on the lap of a parent who was reading or listening to music. Those times are the true foundation for a person's prayer life.

Different people are going to pray in different ways and, as a result, there are many varieties of prayer. There is never one way that is best for all. Many powerful personal and cultural influences are at work in the evolution of our spirituality. Choices in prayer depend more upon personal psychological inclinations, spiritual preferences, and cultural conditioning than on a person's theology.

The shape of windows has been used to explain differing prayer experience. If I am in a hut with round windows, I will experience the morning light differently from any of my neighbors who have square windows or slits or no roofs. There is only one sun, but the shape of my windows (life experiences) determines my awareness and understanding of the sun's light.

It is so important to appreciate the many approaches to prayer that I want to emphasize two spectra, even at the risk of attempting to put the horizonless prayer process in a temporary, analytical box.

Image-to-No Image. For most people, there are a number of basic choices to be made about the process of prayer. Perhaps the first decision concerns mental pictures.

Some like to pray while holding in their minds an image of a god who has a personal relationship with them. This is perhaps the traditional Judeo-Christian method taught to children. There is, however, always a danger of worshiping false gods when we project images of what we want God to be.

At the other end of the scale are those who prefer no images at all. Zen and many other Buddhists would be found here, seeking a mental emptying out that allows a harmonizing with the divine, as a raindrop merges with a lake. Quite a few Christian mystics also assert that God is a "no thing." To them any mental picture is a "thing" we have created ourselves that gets in the way of our pure experience of God.

Cognitive-to-Affective. A second choice to be made in prayer has to do with:

A cognitive, thought-out, intellectual, response as compared with

An affective reaction that incorporates strong feelings and emotions.

Most people are not comfortable at the extreme ends of either the "cognitive-affective" continuum or the "image-no image" one. I tend toward the no-image end but not completely. The affective has more appeal to me than the cognitive, but again I am usually someplace back from the end of the spectrum.

Once we have a general idea of where we are comfortable, we need to combine our preferences and look for some appropriate teachers and writers who will encourage us. I will give a few examples, but there are hundreds more in each situation.

Cognitive/No Image. Those who favor a more cognitive approach and at the same time tend toward emptying out images are going to be nourished by people like Meister Eckhart (1260?-1328) as well as modern day religious philosophers, nature poets, or those who simply like to take walks and reflect on the divine presence in the world.

Cognitive/Image. For those preferring an intellectual approach but with imagery, there is the founder of the Jesuits, Ignatius of Loyola (1491-1556) with his detailed spiritual exercises focusing on God's forgiveness and the life, passion, and resurrection of Christ. Perhaps here is also where we could place some of those today who are concerned with the deeper aspects of psychology and its relationship to spirituality.

Affective/No Image. At the affective end of the scale are powerful feelings of love and sorrow. Today it is popular to combine affective approaches with an emptying out of imagery. The introduction of Buddhist and other Eastern meditative traditions into Western culture has been spiritually refreshing. There is a renewal of interest in the unknown fourteenth-century Christian author of *The Cloud of Unknowing*, and the forms of "centering prayer." where you begin a time of prayer by focusing on a sacred word but move into nothingness and a loving attentiveness to God.

Affective/Image. If an affective preference is combined with images, we would search out writers like Julian of Norwich and Teresa of Avila, who were both deeply involved with vivid imagery. There are many similar guides in all traditions. I have especially benefited from Sufi, Buddhist, Hasidic, Tibetan, Chinese, and Native American teachers and stories.

Many other approaches and combinations of approaches, from Christian and non-Christian traditions, can be nourishing. What is important is that a person understand there is no single or "best" way to pray. We must each find some spiritually comfortable prayer niche, but be ready to modify our approach as we experience changes in our lives and in society.

Contemporary seekers sometimes make a distinction between "prayer" and "meditation." For them, prayer is an active pursuit, usually with words. Meditation is a passive, and wordless, process. This division is not always helpful. The ways in which we touch the divine are as varied as communications between any other lovers.

All of what has been said about prayer so far has been safe for me. Things get a little more rocky when someone asks me "But how do you pray each day?" I have evolved a formula for daily half-hour periods of quiet prayer. It is a program I seldom stick to completely.

I start with a modification on an ancient practice known as *lectio divina*. While beginning with imagery, the process moves on to an emptying out, and uses both cognitive and affective faculties. At least that is how it is supposed to work.

Lectio divina means the divine lesson or reading. It has been used as an approach to prayer in Christian monasteries for over fifteen hundred years. There are many varieties of *lectio divina* other than the one I will share.

Before a period of *lectio* I need a quieting down exercise in which I attempt to restrain or distract the active pursuits of my mind. I often begin by finding a comfortable sitting position and simply listening to the sounds around me. Gradually I become aware of sounds farther away. I try not to get involved with these sounds but let them come and go. The point is to listen to whatever there is to be heard.

At some point, I focus on the sound of my own breathing. I become aware of the air as it comes in and as it goes out. I sometimes remind myself that breathing is a natural process that started at birth. Every breath is an important link in a chain of life. Gradually I fix all my attention on my breathing to the exclusion of everything else. I breathe slowly and deeply. As I breathe, I can feel the air going all the way through my body. With each breath, I attempt to push all the air out. The air will come in naturally, so I concentrate on exhaling. If any thoughts spring up, I simply let them come in and go out.

On rare occasions, there is such a strong sense of rightness that I do not go on; I simply try to remain in that moment. But usually I move on to *lectio*. Or, at least I try to. On some days, I cannot transcend my jumpiness and distractions. I try not to abandon the process on these difficult days. There is an old contemplative adage that says, "Trying to pray is praying."

In its simplest form, *lectio* proper begins by choosing a brief passage. Many texts can be used, biblical and nonbiblical. Sometimes I have used poems, haiku, or a familiar phrase from a psalm such as this from Psalm 84: "How lovely is your dwelling place, Lord God of hosts." Or I use a short episode from the Gospels of Matthew, Mark, or Luke and focus on a specific incident in the life of Jesus. I try not to study the scripture intellectually. I read or repeat the passage a number of times, sometimes aloud, so that my body and my mind are both involved in a process of heightened awareness. Usually the words of the gospel verse drive everything else out of my mind, and for a short time, I am only thinking about a particular moment in the life of Jesus.

Several times I have selected the passage (Luke 4:16-30) where Jesus returned to the synagogue of his native Nazareth after his time of retreat in the desert. As he stood up to read from the Torah, it was obvious he had changed. The words of Isaiah he read took on a new, more intimate meaning:

> He sent me to bring the good news to the poor,
> to proclaim liberty to captives,
> new sight to the blind,
> to set the downtrodden free.

Jesus' neighbors were amazed at his confidence. "Is this not Joseph's son?" they asked. When Jesus claimed that the text he read was going to be fulfilled "today even as you listen," the congregation became enraged. They wanted to throw him over a cliff, but he slipped through them and walked away.

I go over the scene in my imagination until this episode becomes alive for me. I do not consider the passage only a historical event but ponder what it means in my life. I join the synagogue congregation and attempt to open myself to Jesus as he speaks. What is being said? Am I among those who are threatened by him? How do his words relate to my life? This aspect of the process is sometimes given the term *meditatio*. It is an openness to spiritual awareness.

At the most fruitful of times, I sense, despite all my cares, a divine element in my existence. It is hard to reduce this wordless process to words, and is perhaps best to say only that my emotional horizons seem to expand. There is an increased sense of wholeness, which often produces a spontaneous response to my awareness of existing in the universe. My reaction is usually a love or sorrow that comes bubbling up inside of me. This will eventually explode into a simple response without words. *Oratio*, a Latin word for "prayer," is the label given to this part of the lectio process. Then, there can follow an experience which has been called *contemplatio*. For me, when this happens, it is a sweet emptiness in which I surrender to a wordless call and simply rest in the still hands of God for a short time.

I have found *lectio divina* to be a good map that helps me travel to nourishing places. However, there are many times when I just sit down, throw the map away, and listen to the birds.

☀ Issa: Discovering the Milky Way ☀

Adjusting to the destruction of a world we knew and loved is very difficult. But it is not hopeless. Just after the horrors of the First World War, my mother completed a cross-stitch piece of needlework that said, "Earth has no sorrow that heaven cannot heal." It now hangs in the hall outside my bedroom. I have never been able to survive a great loss on my own. I have had the support of heaven and the wisdom of gentle people.

For me one of the great masters of the art of living with loss has been the poet Issa, whom I have cited in this book and, indeed, in all my writings. I deeply respect Issa, not only the haiku poems but the man himself.[19] He had a troubled life in which he was always searching for grace. One poignant poem contains only a few words in the original Japanese: "loveliness," "rip/shoji screen," "milky way." This is what it says to me:

How lovely it is
To look through the broken window
And discover the Milky Way.

Finding the Milky Way after a great loss is not easy, but we should try. Whatever beauty, peace, and harmony Issa found was in the midst of sickness and decay.

Born Yataro Kobayashi, he was two years old when his mother died. Five years later, his father remarried. The new wife disliked and mistreated him. All his life he was to identify with the weak and helpless, be they children, flies, or sparrows.

Come,
you can play with me—
orphaned sparrow.

When Issa was thirteen he went to Tokyo and studied poetry. In his twenties, he committed himself to religion and poetry. It was then he chose the name "Issa," which means a "cup of tea." Like the tea, he saw himself as simple and ordinary. The poetry of this lonely man captured the spiritual isolation of the human condition.

A forty-year-old struggle with his stepmother ended when Issa was fifty. Happy, but in ill health, he was able to return to the village and the old farmhouse where he had been born. He married Kiku, a twenty-seven-year-old village woman. They wanted children badly. Their first child, a boy, died soon after birth. Then, on a day in May, Sato was born. Issa was fifty-seven. "Sato" means "wisdom." It was a good name. Her first year brought much joy. The child was the center of Issa's universe. He rejoiced in every little ordinary but miraculous event of her active life. "She is," he wrote, "moonlight from head to toe . . . ." To live in the presence of such vitality was to experience again the freshness of his life. "Watching her I forget my years and my corrupt past." On his daughter's first birthday Issa contrasted his "meaningless endeavors" with the peace, grace, and joy in Sato's life. "I am ashamed to admit that my little child of one year is closer to the Truth than I am."

Just after Sato's first birthday, Issa took to the road as was the custom for Japanese poets. But a foreboding soon brought him home again. He found Sato seriously ill. A variola virus had attacked, and her immune system was collapsing. She had a very high fever. The frightening signs of smallpox were beginning. Ulcers were covering her beautiful young body. On her recent birthday, Issa had mused that in time she would learn to dance and "her dancing will be lovelier than celestial music!" The little dancer was now struck low. Issa cried out:

> My child is dying. Why? She has just begun to
> taste life and ought to be as fresh and green as

the new needles on the everlasting pine. Why
must she lie here on her deathbed, with festering
lesions, caught in the vile grip of the god of pox?
I am her father and can hardly bear to watch her
fade away, a little more each day, like a pure blossom in a rain storm.

Smallpox plagues claimed millions of victims
over three thousand years. Each statistic was the
destruction of a unique universe of human experiences. So it was with Sato.

She grew weaker until on June 21, as the morning
glories closed their petals, she closed her eyes
forever. Her mother held the cold body and
cried out in unremitting pain.

Emotional attachment was not encouraged in
Issa's spiritual tradition. He had been taught not
to invest his energy in worldly matters that disap-
pear like dew on the grass. But religious doctrines
do not withstand the personal experience of death:
"I tried hard, but I could not break the bonds of
human love." About his loss he wrote:

This world of dew
is nothing but a world of dew,
and yet . . .
and yet . . .

No matter what a person's religious or psychological principles may be, a death adds

and yet ...

and yet ...

In 1820, another son was born to Issa and Kiku, but he died after four months. Two years later a third son was born. The next year Kiku died in May and the boy in December. On November 19, 1827 Issa himself died. He was sixty-four. Shortly before his death, his house burned down. He spent his last days in a storage shed without windows and with holes in the roof. He could see the mid-winter sky. His final poem, found under his pillow, summed up his spiritual quest:

Again, I give thanks—
the snow falling on the bed quilt,
it also comes from God.

Would it have been easier on Issa if Sato and his other children had not been born? Sometimes I hear people suggest things like that. Issa saw it differently. One autumn he wrote:

Deep in my heart
I give thanks to my children,
as the night grows cold.

I have sometimes felt I was stumbling down a path where Issa once walked. Certainly as a writer or spiritual seeker, there can be no comparison. But he was also a father to a little girl. My daughter Tina died in 1991. She was the same age as Sato. Tina died of AIDS. Her little body also was given over to a vile pox. Like Issa, when I was near sixty, I lived under the shadow of a killer virus. And we both walked with a child into the heart of God. It was not an easy journey for either of us.

Issa knew there would have to be a special year in his life after the death of Sato. Soon he resumed his journey. When he returned home again, he wrote *Oraga Haru* or *The Year of My Life*. I was also to have an unparalleled year after Tina's death, but I was not aware of the year, or even of the need for it, until it was over. That seems to be the way it happens to many, if not all, of us. It is, with God's help, a great gift from someone we love.

On family outings I am the one who is hurrying everyone into the car, remembering violins, backpacks, lunches, the dogs, and such. Sometimes I remain behind as the gang goes from our rural home to new adventures in the city. Once the car door is closed, I usually wave exuberantly as they all take off. When I am near death, I hope I can say with my eyes to those I love that it is time to get in the car for there is a very special adventure coming. "Wave goodby to me and take off— for the year of your life."

12

Sacred Circles

Seeing God in others is a difficult matter for me. I frequently look on people as a hindrance to inner peace. Yet it is in the human community that I have most often discovered not only the presence of the sacred but a deeper understanding of my own humanity.

There is a profound mystery about being a person. In the 1960s, the psychologist Carl Rogers (1902-1987) summed up many ideas in the title to his book *On Becoming a Person*. Living is a process of growth—of becoming. Each age has its own problem about becoming a person. In the 1960s the issue for us was seeing ourselves as something more than cogs in the machines of families, churches, professions, businesses, governments. We wanted to be liberated from the expectations of others. The drift after that has been toward individualism. For much of my life, I identified with that flow. I have been and remain greatly influenced by the existentialists, those thinkers who bring all their existence and experience into philosophical, theological, and psychological reflection. However, one of the by-products of this approach has been an epidemic of self-centeredness, so that today I am among those who believe we must liberate ourselves from the self-imposed slavery of a radical individualism.

Community awareness and individualism have see-sawed through history. For example, G.W.F. Hegel (1770-1831) preached a neat comprehensive system in which an Absolute Spirit was the ultimate reality. This sent a troubled Danish philosopher up the wall. Søren Kierkegaard (1813-1855) advocated the intense examination of individual life with all its ambiguity and paradox. Hegel encouraged submission to social duty; Kierkegaard considered this a loss of individual freedom.

In economics, individualists looked on society as an artificiality having merit only to the extent that it helped individual welfare. Collectivists, including the radical revolutionary communists, insisted that the good of the whole must come before the interests of private individuals. The attempt to find a balance between the community and the individual will probably go on forever.

One of the things I have learned is that if I attempt to stand alone in my spiritual growth, I will feel lonely and uncomfortable. Jewish history emphasized the community rather than focusing on each individual person. A particular individual might be off the track, but when the community, the people, were going along alright, that benefited every person in the community. Accepting that each individual was connected to the spiritual well-being of the community meant that everyone accepted some responsibility to help the community be healthy.

When I was a child, Sunday Mass was the center of our spiritual week. I had no doubt that God was there. The bread and wine had become the real presence of Jesus. As an adolescent, I was excited to learn that God was equally present in the people themselves who had gathered for the Mass. As my spiritual experience increased, I became aware that God was present in many human encounters, which were not limited to ritual gatherings. Any meal can be a sacred communion in the tradition of the times when Jesus ate with his friends.

Jesus presided over a family of people, many of whom were not invited to the tables of people who considered themselves respectable. He redefined "family" and became the host at the family table. In the process, he restored the communication between the dejected ones and God. Throughout his ministry, Jesus called everyone to a peaceful fellowship when he broke bread. Sometimes it was with throngs in the open air, and at other times it was in small intimate gatherings. With Jesus, any meal became a divine experience never to be forgotten. At the supper on the night before he was executed, Jesus took bread and wine and said it was his body and his lifeblood. This was a radical way to awaken his friends. Jesus urged them, after he was gone, to gather around the table or altar and to remember that experience. We have been doing it through the centuries. Why? Because we are all spiritually asleep much of the time. Remembering that moment revitalizes us, not just as individuals but as a community.

Jesus gave us a powerful memory through which we can touch some ultimate reality, but he left to us, his sisters and brothers, the responsibility for inviting the whole family to the table. We should do that in a better way than at present where we have separate tables according to people's religious background or beliefs. There should be one table. We can learn from an ancient Christian text, called *The Didache*. Women and men in that community prayed that as the different grains had been gathered from the hills and baked into one bread, "so may your people be gathered from the ends of the earth into your Kingdom." It is still a good prayer. Spiritually we are one people—a people of God.

As previously mentioned, Dietrich Bonhoeffer presented Jesus as a "man for others"—for each one of us. He exists for us today through discipleship, the process of following in his steps by our being for others, not just in the religious subculture but in the secular world as well. Bonhoeffer taught that our God is a suffering God. Jesus was a person "for others" who existed outside the institutional framework of his age. Therefore we too must learn to live a fully human life, which is at the same time a life of service.

Bonhoeffer's life was even more eloquent than his books. His ministry as a German Protestant pastor began as the Nazis were gaining power. American and British friends urged him to remain in New York and London where he had come to teach and serve as a pastor. But when the clouds of war gathered, Bonhoeffer returned to Germany. It was the cost of his Christian discipleship. Bonhoeffer knew it was necessary to join the sacred circle of a suffering people. He opposed Hitler, and was arrested in 1943. Bonhoeffer was brutally executed on April 9, 1945, just a few days before the Allies liberated the camp in which he was held.

Every time I attempt to follow Jesus' words and encounter others around the table or in some other setting, I would like to come with Bonhoeffer's attitude. But I don't. I too often see people only in terms of how they can affect my plans.

There are many jolts in our relationships with people. I heard a story about Sigmund Freud (1856-1939) and the composer Gustav Mahler (1860-1911) meeting on holiday in Holland. Mahler related an incident in which he ran from his Viennese home to escape a scene of domestic violence. As he came onto the street, he encountered a peaceful hurdy-gurdy man playing a pleasant and familiar folk song. Mahler said he experienced the same radical jerk in his sense of existence and in his music. My experience has been similar—except my psyche has usually found peace at home and been knocked around by violence outside. I can be calmly encountering someone after a spiritual service one moment, and the next moment angrily arguing on the phone with an official I believe is too rigid. But there have been times when everything came together for me—at least in the abstract.

On the afternoon of one All Souls Day, November 2, I was sitting on the steps outside our spiritual community's little chapel. It had been a bright autumn day. As the sun moved behind the tops of the redwood trees, there was a slight, but not unpleasant, chill. The other members of the community were sitting nearby. We were listening to a recording of Mozart's *Requiem*.

The chapel is on a hill and I could see for many miles. Just over the hills on the west was the ocean. All the millions of people of the San Francisco Bay Area were somewhere beyond my southern horizon. Under an apple tree to my right were a doe and her fawn.

The "Sanctus" was beginning in the *Requiem* when a large white bird appeared overhead. She flapped her wings rapidly and hovered in the air. I was startled and focused completely on the bird. She would remain in one place for a long time, swing gracefully away and then return to the same spot near me. I knew it was not a special sign from God—nor was it the reincarnation of Wolfgang Amadeus Mozart. The bird was probably simply hunting for field mice. Most likely she came every day. But on this afternoon she led me to a greater awareness of the presence of God in other people.

I was aware of something sacred in the people around me and also in all souls everywhere. This included those racing around in San Francisco and those who rested in the graves near the chapel. It also included the deer under the tree and the bird above. It did not matter how any of us differed from each other. I remembered a Zen scripture that urges us not to separate beings into categories. "Not two! Not two!" it keeps admonishing. Was I being romantic? Perhaps. But my sense of relationship to all beings seemed quite real. We were all one. Differences of values, experiences, lifestyles, and beliefs were all insignificant. In that unity there was God.

As the *Requiem* was coming to the end, I remembered a prayer reflection composed by my son David when he was five. He had been thinking about his little sister who was dying and his grandmother who had died several years before.

When she dies her spirit goes to God.

God is in me.

So, she will be in me.

My grandmother is in me.

There are people in me I don't even know!

There truly are people in each of us we don't even know.

✳ "We Must Be Kin to Each Other" ✳

In any household, there will be major decisions about what we give up in order to get something else. The process of family spiritual growth frequently comes down to a balance between individuality and cooperation. When our family stretched itself to provide an opportunity for David, a gifted child, to receive a musical education in the Bay Area, it was a hardship that required an adult to be away from home on weekdays as well. David understood and accepted that he could not do everything his classmates took for granted. Weekends, for example, were sacred times to be at home. He helped, often in very creative ways, to minimize the disruption. At the same time, David learned that when his dying little sister called out for him to play the violin, as a way of easing her pain, her request took precedence over everything else. It was all a process of giving and receiving gifts. We struggled to help him develop his musical talent. He gave his little sister the gift of that talent. That experience taught him something of the deep potential of music, a quality of David's playing often commented on later. This was his sister's gift to him. At thirteen he received an invitation and a grant to study at The Yehudi Menuhin School in England.

Before the prominence of what we now call the nuclear family, there was a time when bonds of kinship linked families together. It still does in many parts of the globe. The definition of "kin" may change. Usually it means people related by blood or marriage, but not always.

My friend Ben Ssennoga lives in a Ugandan village. Formerly in Ben's world, every possible disaster was handled by the kinship system. There were clear rights and obligations for each degree of relationship to every person. For example, if a child's parents died, there was a definite relative who would immediately welcome the child into her or his hut.

Then the unthinkable happened in Ben's village. AIDS struck. So many people died that one in every nine children was an orphan. Often the child could not go to the appropriate relative's hut because that relative was also dead. The children had no kin. This pained Ben so much that he collected some friends and announced they were kin to anyone without kin. Homes are found. School fees are managed. Clothes and sleeping mats are provided. Birthdays are celebrated. Songs are sung.

Caring hands do what mothers and fathers would have done. They guide the young people toward a nourishing future. Why? As Ben puts it, "We must be kin to each other. We must be!" Ben is an ordinary guy who made his living grinding chicken bones for fertilizer that his neighbors used on their small plots. As folks like Ben work to become kin to the kinless, they provide a welcome echo of Jesus presiding over family meals for those without families and making the dining table a sacred space.

CODA

13

A Spiritual Will

After seventy years on a meandering spiritual journey, I have a growing satisfaction with simply living my life in the confidence that God is with me and us. Many of my struggles with anxiety and fear have been related to a false assumption that my life should be without shocks and troubles. My life is bittersweet—and it is good.

I was born in Mississippi just a few days into 1931. Mississippi was a hate-filled place. My father, recently married, went to the town of Picayune to take up a new job and make a home. When he stepped off the bus, a circle of men were passing a gun around pumping bullets into the corpse of a black man. A horrible sight. My father was even more upset when no one could tell him what the man had done. Why stay in such a town? It was the Depression. He had little choice.

I was born on a Sunday. The old rhyme says, "A child who is born on the Sabbath day is good and kind in every way." It has always been important to me to be seen as "good and kind." And I am—but not "in every way."

One afternoon shortly after I was born, the landlord set fire to our home in order to collect the insurance money. My father saw him looking in the window. He was apparently shocked to find anyone at home. My parents were disgusted with the man but not enraged. They did not complain to the police. Once again, it was the Depression. People do bad things when faced with poverty. We did not have insurance and lost everything. "These things happen," my father would say to me years later.

"These things"—a black corpse, a burning house, the threat of poverty—did not make a good environment for my becoming good and kind in every way. So my parents built a protective wall around me to keep emotional demons out of my spiritual space. I grew up in that enclave and there I had my first experience of God and church. My religion was not a way to understand the world but of shielding me from it. But life within that enclosure was never spiritually cramped.

My mother's parents were French. Grandfather was a Mason and Low-Church Episcopalian from Virginia. My grandmother was a Catholic from southern Louisiana. My favorite aunt was married to John Wesley Reed, the son of a stern Methodist leader from East Texas. My father was Presbyterian, as were all his father's Scotch-Irish family. His mother was a Southern Baptist from Alabama. Catholicism was the main church influence in my life, but it never occurred to me that one person or institution could have the whole truth about God or life. I recall no arguments on religious beliefs. Dogma was not important to my family. How a person encountered God and lived with others was what mattered.

I am not sure what mattered in the church of my infancy; I think it was survival. The Catholic church is at its very best when it is persecuted, and its most disappointing when it is dominant in a society. In Mississippi, we Catholics were on the social margin, ranked on a level with Jews, not outcasts like blacks, but far from the Protestant mainstream. The town marshal was a deacon in one of the big churches. He limped. A friend of my mother recognized that limp when she saw some men in white robes leaving our little church. I can't remember if it was the Ku Klux Klan or the Knights of the White Camellia, but I do recall they all carried axes. They had smashed up our baptismal font. Common adversity is the quickest way to a sense of community. That shattered font, windows broken at the shop of a Jewish neighbor, a dirt floor, and no electricity in a new school built for the town's black kids, suggested to my young mind that we all had something in common. Jews and African-Americans are "ethnic" groups. They have cultures separate from the majority. In the America of my early years, the majority, at least the people with the power, were white Protestants. So it seemed to me that my Catholicism was also an ethnic thing. I am a Catholic because that is my culture.

When my family moved to a small lumber town in Oregon, I went to Mass each Sunday in a rented room above the local bakery. Out the window I could see the figures of Paul Bunyan and his blue ox atop the giant neon sign of the town's most popular bar. There certainly was a frontier feeling about our congregation. That is the feeling I still seek in spiritual associations.

In college, I tried not to be a religious person. I imitated sophisticated agnostic intellectuals on campus, but it was not emotionally satisfying. After law school, I threw myself into making a family and establishing a career. My law practice began in the hysteria of McCarthyism and ended in the struggle for civil rights. It was a challenging time. At the center of my active world were Tamar and Duncan, my first two children, now adults with full lives and children of their own, and my wife, Claire, who struggled with a disabling disease that ultimately took her life.

Eventually I was working with a number of national and international secular causes. In the 1960s I tried to support young people who were striving to make sense out of a world in which we murdered a president, four black girls in a Birmingham Sunday school, and a whole people trying to survive in southeast Asia. Deep spiritual questions were raised that I could not answer. I turned for help to the pioneers of what came to be called "humanistic psychology." My mentors included Rudolf Dreikurs (1897-1972), Abraham Maslow (1908-1970), and other gentle people exploring the psyche.

During this period I met John Courtney Murray (1904-1967), a Jesuit theologian. John had come back from being silenced by the Vatican to author the "Declaration of Religious Liberty" at the Second Vatican Council. He described this document as an "act of humility" by a church that had been a "truant from the school of history." John considered himself a Christian humanist. We had many contacts. Our differences were insignificant compared to our common ground. I was beginning to experience my Christian roots at this point, but I did not know it. I think John did.

Like many others in the 1960s, I put some flowers in my hair and went to San Francisco to participate in the mania we called "the human potential movement." It was the world's greatest carnival. I let my hair grow, exchanged my tie for beads, and bought a Frisbee. Somehow, through all the madness, the definition of what it meant to be human was being expanded.

With some friends, I helped found The Humanist Institute, where we rediscovered bridges between psychology and spirituality. In this setting, we explored the process of spiritual growth in both Eastern and Western traditions. I studied the Tao, Buddhism, and Christian mystics, and became a spiritual coach and writer. Several of us began to consider the possibility of forming a spiritual community. Gentle monks introduced us to the literature and experience of Western monasticism. In time, Marti Aggeler, Julie DeRossi, and I formed the Starcross Monastic Community. We each had a Catholic background and shared a desire to discover the sacred in the ordinary.

In 1976, we permanently established our monastery on a neglected farm in Sonoma County, northwest of the San Francisco Bay Area. My world was filled with plumbing, carpentry, plowing, cows, and trees. And, once again, I was a foster parent and guide to badly neglected or abused children for whom we were providing a permanent home. Several of them, now grown and married, remain part of our extended family.

Slowly Marti, Julie, and I reclaimed our common Catholic heritage and were welcomed by a friendly local bishop. Pope John XXIII (1881-1963) had opened a window to bring fresh air into the church. We were able to gain entrance through the same window. Shortly thereafter it was to be slammed shut.

We have an autonomous relationship with the Catholic hierarchy. Our community, Starcross, has been defined under church law as a pious union or "private association of the Christian faithful." We make the traditional monastic vows, which include poverty and celibacy, but these are considered private understandings with God, not involving official endorsement. However, we have always had a deep fraternal association with monastic communities. Even before the move to the country, there began a long and unique relationship with the Cistercian Abbey of New Clairvaux in Vina, California. The monks, sometimes called "Trappists," have become our primary link to the larger Catholic community. We are family to each other in a formal relationship of spiritual solidarity.

David came into our lives in 1986. His birth mother, a niece of one of us, was very young, overwhelmed at the thought of parenthood, and considering abortion. We joyfully proposed the alternative of adoption. Shortly after David's birth, we became involved with the AIDS pandemic by adopting or becoming guardians for a number of children who were born HIV positive. Of those we adopted, Tina died; Holly and Andrew are now testing negative and no longer have any life-limiting conditions. Each of these children have uniquely contributed to my spiritual life.

In 1990, we provided home care for some previously institutionalized children with AIDS in Romania. In 1997, we were invited to help, spiritually and practically, some of the many children in Uganda orphaned as a consequence of AIDS. I am the godfather for some of these children who are an important part of my life.

There were times in my life when numbers mattered. How many people can I help? How many spiritual roads to peace can I explore? Now, the whole of God, of humanity, of the cosmos, of my life, can be in the experience of one child, one person—one moment.

Wholeness, peace of soul, and spiritual comfort have come to me now mainly in the ordinary moments of daily life. My experience of God comes in a gentle breeze. The places where I have truly opened myself to the divine presence have been next to a sick child, planting a flower, watching a bird, sitting on a train, washing clothes, listening to children making music, cleaning a small chapel. That is the sort of hope I want to leave those who come after me, especially those I love: the understanding that looking at a sunset can change your life, smelling a blossom on a spring morning can make you aware of God, being with someone who is dying can get you splashed with the peace that heaven wraps around those who are leaving us, touching the hand of someone who cares can make us deeply understand the "Good News" of the gospels.

Sacred space, a place where the line between the divine and the human is blurred, has been important to me from my early years. My parents were always worrying about making ends meet. The Depression years had been hard. Life was uncertain. To take a break from this anxiety, my father would turn on his little radio and listen to the evening news. My mother would pray. She was very happy when she prayed. It was a gateway to a holy place, a sanctuary, where she felt at home, safe, and accepted. I grew up keenly sensing the need for such spaces.

I have been many things in my life, but now I am primarily the keeper of a small sacred space. To me, it is a monastery. To my children, it is simply our home. To friends, it is a place of pilgrimage. In this place, large butterflies come in the summer and flocks of birds in the winter. The trees bloom in the spring and turn red in the autumn. Here those I love are born and die. The young must travel away to new places, that they may continue to grow. The older of us are sometimes distracted by illness, but live gently.

When I practiced law I always pushed clients and friends to make wills and insure that the fruits of their labors would go to those they loved. What I have attempted to bequeath in this book are some spiritual stepping stones. They are here for any who can use them. Some of you who are reading this book will have life experiences very different from mine. However, at some deep level, perhaps our individual experiences merge and we can all use what each of us has learned.

There will be many changes in the years to come, presenting challenges that I cannot now imagine. Certainly the century in which I spent most of my life was a time of major turmoil. But I do have hope—and trust you do as well.

In any storm, if we forget everything else, let us pray we remember love. If we simply love each other, truly all shall be well. In the introduction to this book, I mentioned Etty Hillesum.[20] These are the words she wrote to a friend a few weeks before she was murdered at Auschwitz:

> And if we just care enough, God is in safe hands with us despite everything, Maria.

God has said only one thing:
only two do I know —
Psalm 62

Notes

1 Etty Hillesum, *An Interrupted Life* and *Letters from Westerbork*, (New York: Henry Holt and Company, 1996), p.77. This quote is taken from Etty Hillesum's diary entries between 1941-1943. It was originally published in the Netherlands in 1981 as *Het verstoorde leven: Dagboek van Etty Hillesum, 1941-1943*. The English translation of *An Interrupted Life* was made in 1983 by Jonathan Cape Ltd. and published in 1984 by Pantheon Books, a division of Random House, Inc.

2 John Moschos (a.k.a. John Eviratus, A.D. 619), translated by John Wortley, *The Spiritual Meadow (Pratum Spirituale)*, (Kalamazoo, Michigan: Cistercian Publications, 1992), p. 3.

3 There are many editions of this text. All are correct and all are incomplete. My rendition was: *The Tao: The Sacred Way*, (New York: The Crossroad Publishing Company, 1982). Since that time my understanding of The Tao has continued to evolve partly because of other editions and partly because of my own life-experience.

4 Colin Hampton, *A Cellist's Life*, (San Anselmo, California: String Letter Publishing, 2000), p. 87.

5 E.F. Schumacher, *Small is Beautiful: Economics as if People Mattered*, (London: Blond & Briggs Ltd., 1973), (New York: Harper & Row, Publishers, Inc., 1973).

6 Paul Monette, *Borrowed Time: An AIDS Memoir*, (New York: Harcourt Brace Jovanovich, Publishers, 1988); *Becoming a Man; Half a Life Story*, (New York: Harcourt Brace Jovanovich, Publishers, 1992); *Last Watch of the Night: Essays Too Personal and Otherwise*, (New York: Harcourt Brace & Company, 1994, 1993). In addition to these non-fiction works, Paul authored several

books of poetry, six novels, and a number of screenplays. His final work was a fable.

[7] Rainer Marie Rilke, translated by C.F. MacIntyre, *Rilke Selected Poems*, (Berkeley: University of California Press, 1940), p.41.

[8] Christina Yates, *Brother Klaus: Man of Two Worlds*, (York: William Sessions Limited, 1989), pp. 57-59.

[9] Julian of Norwich, translated by James Walsh, *The Revelations of Divine Love*, (St. Meinard, Indiana: Abbey Press, 1974), p. 92.

[10] Rollo May, *Love and Will*, (New York: W.W. Norton & Company, Inc., 1969), p. 81.

[11] Abraham H. Maslow, "Chapter 12: Love in Self-Actualizing People," *Motivation and Personality*, 2nd. edition, (New York: Harper & Row, Publishers, 1970), pp. 181-202.

[12] M. Scott Peck, *The Road Less Traveled: A New Psychology of Love, Traditional Values, and Spiritual Growth*, (New York: Simon & Schuster, Inc., 1978), p. 81.

[13] Carl R. Rogers, *On Becoming a Person: A Therapist's View of Psychotherapy*, (Boston: Houghton Mifflin Company, 1961), p. 185 and passim.

[14] Walker Percy, *The Message in the Bottle: How Queer Man Is, How Queer Language Is, and What One has to Do with the Other*, (New York: Farrar, Straus and Giroux, 1954), p. 116.

[15] Edward Schillebeeckx, translated by Hubert Hoskins, *Jesus: An Experiment in Christology*, (New York: The Seabury Press, 1979), p.674.

[16] Dietrich Bonhoeffer, edited by Eberhard Bethge, translated by Reginald Fuller (revised by Frank Clarke and others), *Letters and Papers from Prison*, (New York: The Macmillan Company, 1967), p. 202. The concept of Jesus as a "man for others" can be found

in many of Bonhoeffer's works, going back to his days as a theological student.

[17] The modern text was written by Eleanor Farjeon. © Copyright David Higham Assoc. Ltd.

[18] Issa, translated by Nobuyuki Yuasa, *The Year of My Life (Oraga Haru)*, 2nd edition, (Berkeley: University of California Press, 1972), p. 127.

[19] Reading, understanding, and writing haiku has been a part of my spiritual life for half-a-century, and yet I have never completely mastered even one poem. Those English versions of poems that I have rendered in this book are the results of insights I have received from many sources. In regard to Issa, I particularly value: Harold G. Henderson, *An Introduction to Haiku: An Anthology of Poems and Poets from Basho to Shiki*, (New York: Doubleday & Company, 1958); Cliff Edwards, *Issa: The Story of a Poet-Priest*, (Tokyo: Macmillian Shuppan KK, 1985); Lewis Mackenzie, *The Autumn Wind: A Selection from the Poems of Issa*, (London: John Murray Ltd., 1957); *Issa, The Year of My Life*, op. cit. The life story and poems in this chapter are also presented in: *Issa, The Year of My Life*, op. cit., pp. 93-95, 103-104, and, Cliff Edwards, Issa, op. cit., pp. 41-43.

[20] Etty Hillesum, *An Interrupted Life and Letters from Westerbork*, op. cit., p. 359. This quote is taken from Etty Hillesum's letters originally published in the Netherlands in 1982 as *Het denkende hart van de barak*. The first English translation was made by Random House, Inc. and published in 1986 by Pantheon Books, a division of Random House, Inc.

With Grateful Thanks

In the writing of this book I was bolstered by the encouragement and inspiration of many people. Five friends played unique roles in the process. Shortly before he died, Paul Monette asked me to write the book. He made a strong, and persistent, case. Talented friends helped me shape the work. Jan-Erik Guerth has been as much an editor as an agent. He vigorously represented the potential readers Paul had envisioned. I will always remember one two-hour phone conversation when Jan-Erik called from a rickety phone booth in the middle of the desert. Sitting on the dirt floor, and reading by the light of the full moon, he went over every page of the manuscript! Roy M. Carlisle, my editor at PageMill Press, intertwined his long years in publishing with his personal experience as a spiritual seeker to make excellent suggestions on how I could better present what I had written. Marti Aggeler and Julie DeRossi, my sisters in the Starcross Community, have for more than thirty years worked to craft the spiritual environment within which all of the experience in this book has emerged. Beyond that, they have taken many hours to read and reread draft after draft with helpful criticisms and affirmation. They were always there to help with everything from punctuation to proofreading, often late at night after their many other tasks of the day. They, together with all the friends and supporters of Starcross Community, have made it possible for me to have the opportunity to write. The limitations of this book represent my inability to take full advantage of the generous and gracious help offered by many wonderful people.

Grateful acknowledgment is made to the following for permission to reprint previously published material.

The quote of Etty Hillesum in the introduction is from *An Interrupted Life*. English translation copyright © 1983 by Jonathan Cape Ltd. Reprinted by permission of Pantheon Books, a division of Random House, Inc. The quote in the final chapter is from *Letters from Westerbork*. English translation copyright © 1986 by Random House, Inc. Reprinted by permission of Pantheon Books, a division of Random House, Inc.

Excerpts from "My Priest" and "3275" in *Last Watch of The Night*, copyright © 1994, 1993 by Paul Monette, Trustee, and his successor Trustee/s of the Monette/Horwitz Trust u/I 2/12/92, reprinted by permission of Harcourt, Inc. The four lines of Rainer Maria Rilke's poem "Erinnerung" are found in *Rilke Selected Poems*. English translation copyright © 1940 by C. F. MacIntyre (University of California Press). Reprinted by permission of the Regents of the University of California. Also, Issa's haiku, "In the autumn wind . . .," appears as it was translated by Nobuyuki Yuasa in *The Year of My Life (Oraga Haru)*, 2nd edition, Copyright © 1972 by The Regents of the University of California (University of California Press). Reprinted by permission of the Regents of the University of California, 1972

All quotes from scripture are excerpted from The Jerusalem Bible, copyright © 1966 by Darton, Longman & Todd, Ltd. and Doubleday, a division of Random House, Inc. Reprinted by permission.

About the Author

Tolbert McCarroll, known as "Brother Toby," is a monk at Starcross, a small lay-community in the Catholic monastic tradition. He is the adoptive father of three young children, and lives on a farm in the western hills of Sonoma County. Toby prefers to spend his time planting olive trees, listening to music, writing, and exploring life with his community and his children. A former attorney for human causes, he still frequently ventures forth in response to children in need. This he has done in California, Romania, and Uganda where he established homes for children oppressed by the AIDS pandemic. This book, his eighth, draws from Toby's rich life experiences to provide a spiritual will and testament to people of every faith, and of none.

About the Press

"...the language of the wise brings healing."
Proverbs 12:18b

At PageMill Press, we publish books that explore and celebrate the Christian life. Our titles cover a wide range of topics including spiritual memoir, devotional and contemplative life, peace and justice issues, faith-based community work, spiritual disciplines, reference works, family and parenting, spirituality, and fiction.

We believe that publishing involves a partnership between author, publisher, the bookseller, and the reader. Our commitment as a publisher to this partnership is to produce wise and accessible books for thoughtful seekers across the full spectrum of the Christian tradition.

The Press seeks to honor the writer's craft by nurturing the felicitous use of language and the creative expression of ideas. We regard highly the collaboration of publisher, editor, and author, and the creative expression of ideas with the knowledge and wisdom that results.

For a catalogue of publications of PageMill Press, for editorial submissions, or for queries to the author, please direct correspondence to:

PageMill Press
2716 Ninth Street
Berkeley, CA 94710
Ph: 510-848-3600; Fax: 510-848-1326